Editor
Lorin Klistoff

Editor in Chief
Karen J. Goldfluss, M.S. Ed.

Cover Artist
Tony Carrillo

Art Production Manager
Kevin Barnes

Imaging
Leonard P. Swierski

Publisher
Mary D. Smith, M.S. Ed.

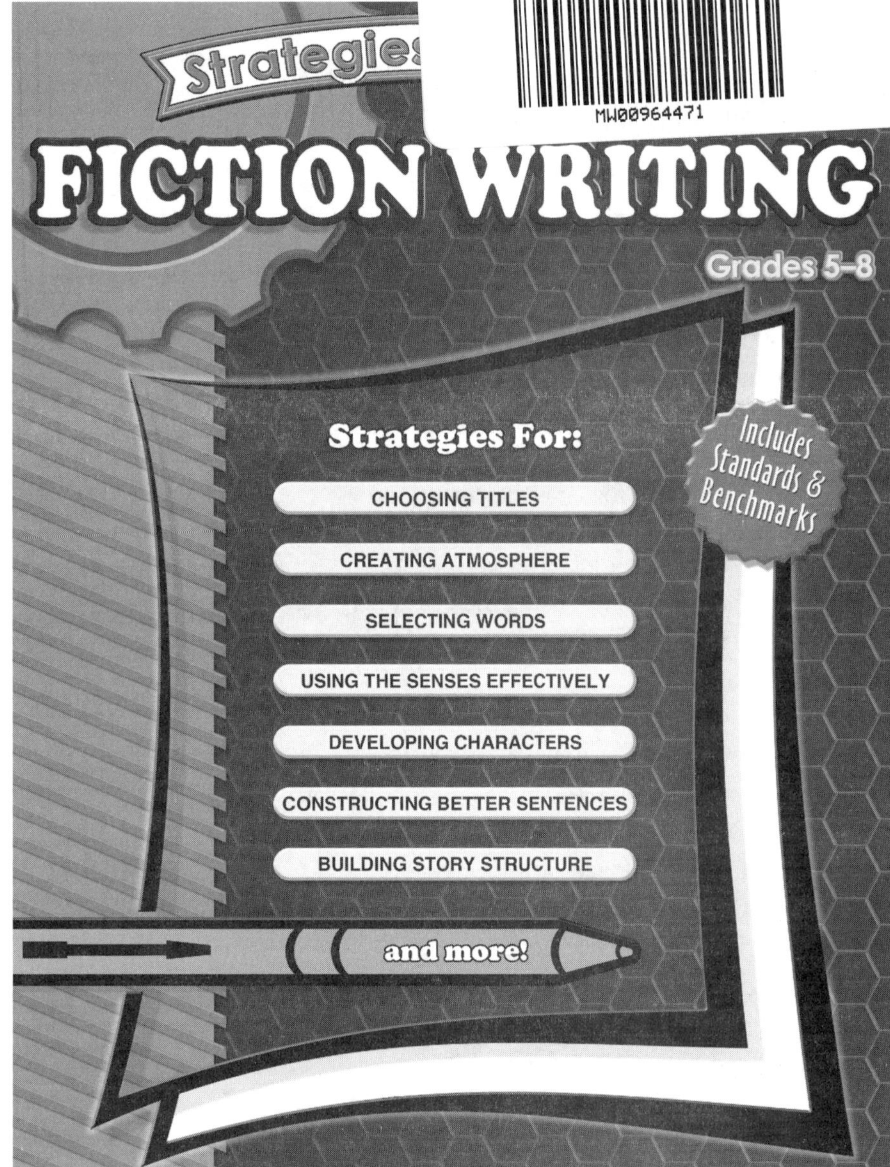

Author
Alan Horsfield

Teacher Created Resources, Inc.
6421 Industry Way
Westminster, CA 92683
www.teachercreated.com
ISBN: 978-1-4206-8056-0

Made in U.S.A.

Table of Contents

About the Author

Alan Horsfield taught for many years in schools across New South Wales, Australia. In 1980 he went to Papua New Guinea as principal of an international school. In the early 1990s he returned to Australia to resume teaching in the eastern suburbs of Sydney.

On leaving teaching he began to write children's textbooks and children's stories. He ran a series of writing workshops in Sydney and in other areas of New South Wales.

In 1994 he became president of the New South Wales Children's Book Council. He has been a judge for the New South Wales Premier's Book Awards and spent two years working at the University of New South Wales as an English Research Officer, before moving to Fiji to concentrate on writing.

Alan is now living in Sydney where he still runs writing workshops for primary and secondary students. He has written over fifty books. Many of them are textbooks but a considerable number are children's fiction. He has won prizes for writing and has been published around the world.

Standard 1: Uses the general skills and strategies of the writing process

Level III (Grades 6–8)

1. Prewriting: Uses a variety of prewriting strategies (Pages: 11–17, 118, 119, 152, 153, 155, 156)
2. Drafting and Revising: Uses a variety of strategies to draft and revise written work (Pages: 37–41)
3. Editing and Publishing: Uses a variety of strategies to edit and publish written work (Pages: 117–129, 149–156)
4. Evaluates own and others' writing (Pages: 7–158)
5. Uses content, style, and structure appropriate for specific audiences and purposes (Pages: 9, 10, 19, 32, 93–96)
7. Writes narrative accounts, such as short stories (Pages: 7–158)
11. Writes compositions that address problems/solutions (Pages: 30, 117–124)
12. Writes in response to literature (Pages: 7–158)

Level IV (Grades 9–12)

1. Prewriting: Uses a variety of prewriting strategies (Pages: 11–17, 118, 119, 152, 153, 155, 156)
2. Drafting and Revising: Uses a variety of strategies to draft and revise written work (Pages: 37–41)
3. Editing and Publishing: Uses a variety of strategies to edit and publish written work (Pages: 117–129, 149–156)
4. Evaluates own and others' writing (Pages: 7–158)
5. Uses strategies to address writing to different audiences (Pages: 9, 10, 19, 32, 93–96)
6. Uses strategies to adapt writing for different purposes (Pages: 138–140)
8. Writes fictional, biographical, autobiographical, and observational narrative compositions (Pages: 7–158)
9. Writes persuasive compositions that address problems/ solutions or causes/effects (Pages: 30, 117–124)
10. Writes descriptive compositions (Pages: 55–76)
12. Writes in response to literature (Pages: 7–158)

Standard 2: Uses the stylistic and rhetorical aspects of writing

Level III (Grades 6–8)

1. Uses descriptive language that clarifies and enhances ideas (Pages: 55–76, 81–84, 130–137)
2. Uses paragraph form in writing (Pages: 26–32, 155, 156)
3. Uses a variety of sentence structures to expand and embed ideas (Pages: 9, 10, 37–41, 43–54, 151)

Level IV (Grades 9–12)

1. Uses precise and descriptive language that clarifies and enhances ideas and supports different purposes (Pages: 55–76, 81–84, 130–137)
2. Uses paragraph form in writing (Pages: 26–32, 155, 156)
3. Uses a variety of sentence structures and lengths (Pages: 9, 10, 37–41, 43–54, 151)
5. Uses a variety of techniques to provide supporting detail (Pages: 22–25)
6. Organizes ideas to achieve cohesion in writing (Pages: 7–158)
7. Uses a variety of techniques to convey a personal style and voice (Pages: 7–158)

Standard 3: Uses grammatical and mechanical conventions in written compositions

Level III (Grades 6-8)

1. Uses pronouns in written compositions (Pages: 47–50, 97–100, 124)
2. Uses nouns in written compositions (Pages: 47–50, 126)
3. Uses verbs in written compositions (Pages: 47–50, 93–96, 101–116, 144–148, 151)
4. Uses adjectives in written compositions (Pages: 47–50, 55–76, 144–148, 151)
5. Uses adverbs in written compositions (Pages: 47–50, 126, 144–148, 151)
6. Uses prepositions and coordinating conjunctions in written compositions (Pages: 44, 47–50, 124)
10. Uses conventions of punctuation in written compositions (Pages: 38–40)
11. Uses appropriate format in written compositions (Pages: 7–158)

Level IV (Grades 9–12)

1. Uses pronouns in written compositions (Pages: 47–50, 97–100, 124)
2. Uses nouns in written compositions (Pages: 47–50, 126)
3. Uses verbs in written compositions (Pages: 47–50, 93–96, 101–116, 144–148, 151)
4. Uses adjectives in written compositions (Pages: 47–50, 55–76, 144–148, 151)
5. Uses adverbs in written compositions (Pages: 47–50, 126, 144–148, 151)
6. Uses conjunctions in written compositions (Pages: 44, 47–50, 124)
9. Uses conventions of punctuation in written compositions (Pages: 38–40)
11. Uses standard format in written compositions (Pages: 7–158)

Standard 4: Gathers and uses information for research purposes

Level III (Grades 6–8)

1. Uses a variety of strategies to plan research (Pages: 16, 17)
3. Uses a variety of resource materials to gather information for research topics (Pages: 16, 17)
4. Determines the appropriateness of an information source for a research topic (Pages: 16, 17)

Level IV (Grades 9–12)

2. Uses a variety of print and electronic sources to gather information for research topics (Pages: 16, 17)
3. Uses a variety of resource materials to gather information for research topics (Pages: 16, 17)

References

Extracts from the following works have been included in this book:

Aitutaki Phantom, Alan Horsfield, Thomson Learning Australia, 2000.

Bubble Buster, Alan Horsfield, Blake Education (Sparklers), 1998.

Cadaver Dog, Alan Horsfield, Lothian Books, 2003.

Charlotte's Web, E.B. White, Puffin Books, 1963.

"Dream On, Brian," Alan Horsfield, from *Dreams* selected by Stephen Matthews, Ginninderra Press, 2002.

Freddie the Frightened, Pamela Shrapnel, Angus & Robertson, 1988.

Harley, Alan and Elaine Horsfield (Unpublished).

Holly and the Frog Prince, Elaine Horsfield, Learning Media Ltd., NZ, 1999.

Sit Down, Mom, There's Something I've Got to Tell You, Moya Simons, Penguin Group Australia, 1995.

Spooked!, Errol Broome, HBJ Spectrum, 1992.

"Streetscape," Ian Steep, from *Through the Web and Other Stories*, HBJ Spectrum, 1992.

Sounder, William H. Armstrong, Puffin Books, 1982.

Talking in Whispers, James Watson, Fontana Lions, 1985.

The Big Race, Alan Horsfield, Thomson Learning Australia, 1997.

The Black Tower, P.D. James, Sphere Books, 1977.

The Ghost Writer, Alan Horsfield, Macmillan Education Australia, 1997.

The Kidnapping of Susie Q, Catherine Sefton, Hamish Hamilton, London, 1994.

The Rats of Wolfe Island, Alan Horsfield, Lothian Books, 2002.

The Strange Story of Elmer Floyd, Alan Horsfield, Longman Pearson, 2002.

"The Train," poet/source not known

Thinks, David Lodge, Martin Secker & Warburg, reprinted by permission of The Random House Group Ltd., London, 2002

Unreal!, Paul Jennings, Penguin Group Australia, 1985.

"Zeppo," Virginia King, from *Through the Web and Other Stories*, HBJ Spectrum, 1992.

Strategies That Work!: Fiction Writing is a practical guide to writing fiction. It looks at those skills required to write better fiction–ways to make students' writing more appealing and interesting. The activities in this book provide scores of writing samples, tips, and practice opportunities to help students improve their writing.

The unit topics are as follows:

- writing fiction (narratives)
- recognizing where ideas for stories come from
- writing what you know
- choosing titles
- know the importance of detail
- creating opening paragraphs
- writing closing paragraphs
- adding closing sentences
- using different sentence types
- explaining rhetorical questions
- using variety in sentence length
- using variety in sentence beginnings
- using repetition
- using all the senses
- selecting direct or indirect speech
- creating characters
- giving characters names
- giving characters real character
- showing, not telling
- selecting a point of view
- finding other words for *say*, *look*, and *go*
- structuring a story
- using metaphors, similes, and clichés
- adding personification and hyperbole
- using different text types
- developing a "What if?" element
- creating atmosphere
- starting a "good word" list
- looking at features of a story
- responding to a prompt
- using a checklist for story writing

The self-contained units cover significant features of fiction writing in depth and extend students' writing ability by providing plenty of practical advice and suggestions for further development. Since each unit can be taught independently, it is not necessary to work through the units sequentially. Choose the topics or the order of presentation that best meets your students' needs. Or, tailor your writing program further by selecting specific units for individual students or groups needing extra practice with a skill.

The text is written in an easy-to-read format that makes learning the techniques of fiction writing an enjoyable experience for students. On occasion, information for the reader is presented in the first person. In these instances, the author provides insight, inspiration, and other valuable writing tips and examples in a way that is both reader-friendly and practical.

Additional features at the back of this book include a page of helpful tips for aspiring writers and an answer key for the unit exercises. Where specific responses are not applicable, suggested answers have been provided in the answer key.

This book is not intended to teach you about correct punctuation, grammar, parts of speech, spelling, or text types. Instead, it is a practical guide to writing fiction (narratives, stories). It looks at the various skills required to write better fiction–ways to make your writing more appealing and more interesting.

The skills are introduced with some explanation where necessary or some quick revision of the practical knowledge required to implement the skill. There are practical exercises to work. Wherever possible, extracts from published stories have been included as examples of how it can be done.

However, just reading the book and the extracts and doing the exercises will not make you a better writer. Like all skills, they have to be practiced. A volleyball player or a soccer player doesn't just know the rules and develop an understanding of how to play the game, they get out there and practice. Just as with any skill, the more you practice, the better you become. Runners run nearly every day. Serious writers write nearly every day.

The biggest problem in writing is procrastination–putting-off getting started. The only way to defeat procrastination is to actually start writing. The first few words or sentences may seem artificial or even corny, but once most people start writing, the words begin to flow with greater ease. Think of the runner taking his or her first training paces. He or she may be reluctant to start, but once he or she has started, the runner finds a rhythm, and it becomes easier.

Words of Advice

First, don't be afraid to let other people read your stories. Stories are meant to be "published." When you are aware that others will be reading or listening to your creative efforts, you become more critical of the words you use and the way your story unfolds. It keeps you on your toes, so to speak. Reading stories aloud to an audience (even an audience of one) gives you a chance to make corrections, amendments, and improvements to your work.

Second, remember to treat your readers as intelligent, imaginative people who also have had experience that they will bring to your writing. Don't try to spoon feed them. Let them use their imagination and experiences when reading your stories. There is a section in the book that helps you do this (Chapter 23: Showing, not Telling).

Keep writing and let your imagination run free.

What is a **narrative**? It is a way of telling a story. The story may be a fable or fantasy. It may be historical or imagined. It may be a play or a poem. In this book the emphasis is on **fiction writing**. Chapters 28 and 29 detail the structure of narratives.

A narrative is not a recount. The main purpose of a **recount** is to retell past events or experiences. Recounts usually retell events in the order they happened.

Narratives do more than retelling a series of events. They try to create experiences that are shared with the reader. The writer uses many literary techniques to capture the reader's attention. This book will introduce you to some of these techniques.

Exercise A

(answer page 162)

Read these two extracts and decide which is a recount and which is a narrative. Write your choice in the space underneath each extract.

Extract 1

At a few minutes after six in the morning, the rain started. The campers quickly put their belongings into tents or rolled them up in sheets of blue canvas.

It rained for more than fifty minutes before there was a break in the clouds.

By this time the younger children were hungry and crying and the older children were looking very bored.

By seven o'clock some of the camp organizers had a hasty meeting to plan a new set of beach events for the morning's activities.

____

Extract 2

Just when the sun should have been peeping over the horizon, heavy black clouds rolled in from the sea and cloaked the camp in half-light.

Then the rain started. Not just a summer shower but a downpour. A downpour so heavy it sent the campers scurrying for shelter and their belongings. Things were thrown into tents or hastily rolled up in gaudy blue plastic.

Then everyone waited–and waited.

The Murdoch's baby started crying like an upset and neglected kitten.

____

Read the opening sentences again and consider the differences.

Text type	Features
Recount (Extract 1)	Retells past experiences and events. It sets the actual time and who is involved.
Narrative (Extract 2)	Creates a word picture of the situation and is part of a story.

EXERCISE B

(answer page 162)

Read the narrative extract on page 1 and select five words that the writer used to make the writing more vivid and appealing.

________, ________, ________, ________, ________

EXERCISE C

(answer page 162)

Read this short personal recount and rewrite the beginning as a narrative. Remember to use words imaginatively.

> On the Monday after Easter our family rose early, had a hurried breakfast, and gathered on the front lawn. We were all excited as we waited for the car that Dad had won in an art contest to arrive.
>
> When a bright red Holden came around the corner into our street, we all cheered.
>
> The car pulled up to the curb in front of our house, and we all dashed through the front gate for a closer look.
>
> Mr. and Mrs. Williams were on their small front porch to watch the excitement.

FEATURES OF NARRATIVES

- Narratives generally use **direct speech** (that is, what is actually said is in quotes) whereas recounts make greater use of indirect speech (e.g., Tom said that he thought the wind would change.)
- Narratives may use **incomplete sentences**. Words and phrases are used for impact.
- Narratives contain facts, descriptions, and **atmosphere**. (Atmosphere is the "feeling" a story—a book or film—creates in the reader's mind/imagination.) Narratives are often designed to **entertain**.

FEATURES OF RECOUNTS

- Recounts are usually in **past tense** (time) whereas narratives have more flexibility in their use of tense.
- Recounts record actual **facts** and events, and are used in articles and personal letters.
- Recounts tend to use complete sentences and are often designed to **inform**.

EXERCISE D

(answer page 162)

Highlight two or three of the narrative features mentioned above in this extract.

> Another night without lights. The power had been off for three days, and Jan was again sitting in the dark house. Alone. Branches scraped against the windowpanes with eerie screeches with each gush of wind. She had heard it a dozen times, and she jumped with each new sound. She was becoming frazzled and scared.
>
> There was a sudden knocking on the front door or on the wooden wall of the tired old house.
>
> "Who's there?" she called nervously, without thinking.
>
> She realized her mistake immediately.
>
> She waited, almost holding her breath.
>
> No reply.
>
> No more knocks.
>
> Maybe it had been her imagination. Maybe not.
>
> Slowly, ever so slowly, she pushed herself up from the warm cushions of her grandfather's old lounge chair and crept towards the rectangle of gray glass next to the front door.

EXERCISE E

(answer page 162)

Highlight two or three of the narrative features mentioned on the previous page in this extract.

Kon became aware that something was going to happen.

Everyone was staring at him, but when he took a closer look, they were watching something going on behind his back. Looking right past his sandy hair to something in the distance. Well, not too distant.

Slowly, he turned his head. Dee Song giggled and tried to cover her mouth with her hand. Then there was an explosion, so loud and unexpected that he fell backwards off his bench seat as Dee cried, "Gotcha!"

All the kids laughed loudly. Rusty Irons jumped up and down, slapping his hips as if he were a demented monkey.

Kon looked back to where the sound had come from.

There was Kylie pulling a splat of pink bubble gum off her face. Kon guessed it was nearly as big as a small pizza–but didn't look as appetizing. She was pushing it back into her mouth and trying not to laugh at the same time.

Kon got up off the gym floor and scuffed to the double doors, then outside. Big joke!

Writers on school visits are often asked where they get their ideas for stories. There is no easy answer to this question. There is no secret either.

Once you start writing with zeal, and you want to keep writing–ideas will pop up everywhere. They come at the most unexpected times. That is why many writers carry a small notepad and pen, or even laptop computers with them wherever they go. Some even have pen and paper beside the bed.

Where Ideas Come From

This is just a sample of where ideas can come from:

- TV shows
- things that happen in the family
- things that happen at school
- newspapers and magazine articles
- other books
- conversations and chance remarks

And sometimes ideas seem to come in a flash from nowhere.

The idea for a story may be a simple incident but the writer sees in it the possibility for a story. The incident grabs the writer's imagination. This does not mean that the writer rushes to his or her office and starts furiously typing a complete story.

Most likely, the idea sits in the writer's imagination and bits of the story start falling into place–the setting, the character, the plot, the detail, the ending. Some writers liken this process to a seed growing in the garden. There are many seeds in our gardens. Some will be flowers, others will be weeds, and some won't germinate at all.

Inspiration for Stories

My idea for *The Big Race* came from a school sports day as I watched the kids in a mini-marathon. I knew what must have been going through their minds as I had just competed in the Sydney City to Surf Fun Run. I didn't write the story until much later, but the idea was there all the time–not always at the front of my mind by certainly in my little notebook.

The idea for *Cadaver Dog* came to me at an international airport as I watched "sniffer" dogs check the passengers' luggage. This reminded me of all sorts of specially trained police dogs. I didn't use the airport as the setting but rather a combination of isolated schools I had once taught in. I wrote the story many years later.

Writing Tip

Keep a notebook for story ideas. They won't always turn into stories, but they are there in black and white if you ever get the urge and inspiration to develop the ideas.

Write down one or two exciting story ideas you have had recently.

____

____

TAKING IDEAS TO PLOTS

From ideas come plots. Don't discard your ideas too readily. One day, in some flash of inspiration, you might just have a prize-winning story.

My little ideas book has over fifty story ideas–most of which I will probably never use. However, I found it comforting to have written down the ideas and avoided the frustration of forgetting them. Sometimes an idea seems fantastic to begin with, and then, the more you think about it, the more difficult (or nonsense) it seems.

Here are a few ideas from my book. I had no ideas about the characters or the plots for these stories. It's just that at one time I liked the ideas.

1. Hidden cell phone found ringing near a bank (mystery)
2. A tattoo that comes to life (horror/fantasy)
3. Clockwork mice versus battery-driven mice race (humorous action)
4. A pink (or another color) snowman (humorous)
5. A Santa Claus convention (humorous)
6. A young, misguided Cupid (humorous)

As you can see, the ideas are quite strange, but there is a bit of a story in each that may be developed at a later date.

EXERCISE B

Start your own list of story ideas. Don't worry if they sound silly.

1. ______________________________
2. ______________________________
3. ______________________________
4. ______________________________
5. ______________________________
6. ______________________________
7. ______________________________
8. ______________________________
9. ______________________________
10. ______________________________

The inspiration for the story *Daily Bread* came to me when my wife started experimenting with different types of bread in her new breadmaker.

Writing Tip

Remember, many stories start with simple ideas that can be developed with a little imagination. Keep a file of your ideas on hand. You never know when they may inspire a great story!

3 WRITING WHAT YOU KNOW— FIRST-HAND EXPERIENCES

Many good stories draw heavily on the **experiences** of the writer. A story you write about happening in your home, street, or town will have a more authentic ring than, say, a story set in Moscow or New York, if you have never been there.

One of my more successful books (*The Rats of Wolfe Island*) was set in Fiji—just down the road from where I lived. I could check out the "concrete" detail regularly. No doubt, to readers in Alice Springs or Arizona, the setting is exotic. To me, it was a commonplace and ordinary. I had stories set in the Cook Islands, outback New South Wales, the inner suburbs of Sydney—and they are all places where I had lived or worked.

Don't be embarrassed by the fact that your setting is pretty ordinary. If the story is well written, then the setting will be interesting to the reader. It's most likely the reader doesn't know your setting intimately, so it will be new to that reader.

Writing Tip

Write about life experiences. Write about what's happening in your world everyday.

EXPERIENCE COUNTS

Many recognized writers are older adults who have had a variety of life experiences. It can be difficult to write about love, death, loneliness, and rejection if you have never experienced them.

However, older people may be out of touch with what's happening in the real world of younger people. As a younger writer, you may be better able to convey these ideas.

EXERCISE A

Make a list of specific places you could write about with some confidence (e.g., shopping mall, vacation place).

______________________ ______________________

______________________ ______________________

______________________ ______________________

______________________ ______________________

______________________ ______________________

EXERCISE B

Make a list of experiences you could write about with some confidence (e.g., winning or losing a sporting match, being home alone, getting lost).

EXERCISE C

Make a list of feelings you could write about with some confidence (e.g., excitement, disappointment, frustration).

EXERCISE D

Make a list of characters you could write about with some confidence (e.g., bully, grandparent, enthusiastic teacher).

First-hand and Secondary Experiences

When I wrote the story *Monopillar*, I took quite a few trips on the Sydney monorail, taking notes. The basic setting for the story was the monorail. I went after the first-hand experience I needed.

Because of your subject matter, however, you might have to write about something you haven't experienced. For *The Ghost Writer,* I had to know something about voodoo, so I went to the local library and looked up books on voodoo to find secondary experiences.

Nowadays information is readily available from many sources, including the Internet.

EXERCISE E

(answer page 162)

List places where you may find useful information for a story you want to research.

Writing Tip

Start at home with parents (and grandparents) and people close to your family.

ALWAYS CHECK YOUR SOURCES

Take care with information from any source. If you are not sure of the difference between, say, a possum and a squirrel, and you don't bother to check it out, you can bet that some of your story will be "full of holes."

Don't use words you aren't fully sure of and hope that the readers will forgive you for your ignorance. They won't!

What is the difference between a possum and a squirrel? (The answer is on page 162.)

EXERCISE F

Write a few sentences about an incident that occurred at your home or school. Remember, you are writing a narrative, not a recount or a report.

EXERCISE G

Research one of the following topics and write a brief fiction passage based on your research. (If you have another topic you would rather research, you may use that topic.)

Suggested topics: skydiving, bungee jumping, mud wrestling

Topic researched: ______________________________

4 Choosing Titles (What's in a Name?)

The title of a story is important because it:

- → suggests the subject matter of the story
- → suggests the kind of story
- → gives a clue to the tone or style of writing
- → may even suggest the age group of the reader

For example, what does the children's book *Valley of Gold* (Jackie French) suggest?

Subject: gold mining/prospecting

Kind of story: Outdoor adventure

Tone or style: Historical

Age group: Upper primary readers

EXERCISE A

(answer page 162)

What does the title *The Frog Princess* (A.D. Baker) suggest to you?

Subject: ____________________

Kind of story: ____________________

Tone or style: ____________________

Age group: ____________________

There are times when you have to read part of the story before the reason for the title becomes obvious.

EXERCISE B

For many school exercises, the teacher provides the title. In free choice writing or even writing for a competition, you may be required to provide your own title. Many competitions just give a general theme. In one competition for children's stories the theme was "Dreams." My entry was titled "Dream on, Brian!"

1. What suggestion do you have for a serious entry on a dream theme?

____

2. What suggestion do you have for a humorous entry on a dream theme?

____

EXERCISE C

(answer page 162)

What age group do you think a story with the title *Professor Iggle and the Dog Walking Machine* is suitable for? ______________________

EXERCISE D

Write a short fictional piece (or a small part of a story) using the title *Professor Iggle and the Dog Walking Machine.*

____

____

____

____

____

____

____

____

____

____

____

____

____

____

____

____

Writing Tip

Many writers can't begin writing until they have a title. My suggestion is to start writing and worry about the title later. Sometimes it suddenly pops out at you. In one of my earlier stories, the title was the last line of the story: "So Much for Aliens!" It is best if the title can entice the reader to find out more about your story.

Techniques for Creating Titles

Single-Word Titles

Moonstorm (Kim Wilkins)
Monopillar (A. Horsfield)
Dingo
Stranded (Jan Thorburn)
Blubber (Judy Blume)

Exclamation Titles

What a Goat! (Errol Broome)
Relax Max! (Brian Caswell)
Lookout!
Bombs Away!
Titans! (M. Stephens)

Unusual Mixtures

The Green Wind (T. Fowler)
Skating on Sand (Libby Gleeson)
Stone Baby (Beth Norling)
Man Bites Dog (Adam Ford)

Descriptions

The Girl from Glenrock
The Rats of Wolfe Island (A. Horsfield)
The Secret Beach (Jackie French)
Treasure Island (R.L. Stevenson)

Alliteration

Desert Dog (Pat Lowe)
Bubble Buster (A. Horsfield)
My Sad Skeleton (A. Horsfield)
Chadwick's Chimney (Colin Thiele)

Rhymes

Jinx the Linx
Neat Beat
Frank's Pranks
Cat in the Hat (Dr. Seuss)
Staying Alive in Year Five (John Marsden)

Contrasts

Beggars' Bank
Summer Snow
Silent Bells
Frozen Fire (James Houston)

Puns (Word Plays)

Sherlock Bones (Con Brecon)
Two Weeks with the Queen (M. Gleitzman)
Slay Ride
Dead on Time

Questions

Who Stole the Tarts?
What About Tomorrow? (Ivan Southall)

Amusing Titles

Unreal Banana Peel (June Factor)
The Cabbage Patch Fib (Paul Jennings)

Teasers

Sit Down, Mom, There's Something I've Got to Tell You (Moya Simons)
The Best Kept Secret (Emily Rodda)

Two of Alan Horsfield's Favorites

Dreamslip (Brian Caswell)
Dear Nobody (Berlie Doherty)

EXERCISE E

List five titles you thought were clever.

1. ______________________________
2. ______________________________
3. ______________________________
4. ______________________________
5. ______________________________

EXERCISE F

(suggested answers page 162)

Create titles for these children's stories. Use some of the techniques listed above.

A clown commits a crime ____________________

Children trapped on an iceberg ____________________

A rescue from a cave-in ____________________

The life of a snowman ____________________

A talking parrot is let loose in a church ____________________

EXERCISE G

Add your own titles to this table.

Single-Word Titles	Exclamations	Unusual Mixtures	Descriptions	Alliteration

Writing Tip

Keep a list in your ideas book of titles you like or have created. It is so easy to forget ideas if you don't write them down. Start a temporary list here.

Knowing the Importance of Detail—Concrete or General?

Using **concrete detail** can lift a piece of story writing from the mundane to the visually exciting. Concrete detail is very specific—don't just mention a cold drink, say a pink lemonade!

READING TASK

Compare these three paragraphs to see what differences the detail makes.

1. It was a warm day. Jo had taken off her jacket and was finding a spot on the track to do some pre-game warm-up exercises. After a few moments of running on the spot, she started sweating on her forehead. She stopped for a moment to get water from her bag.
2. It was warm spring day, more than 85 degrees. Jo removed her tracksuit top as she gazed around the track for a spot to do some jogging and pre-game stretches. A few minutes jogging and she was sweating. She found her sports bag, took a plastic bottle of water from it and had a few sips.
3. Jo was hot by the time she reached the racing track–it was at least 85 degrees. She gazed unhappily about the grounds. She needed space for some jogging and some pre-match stretches without onlookers. Finding a spot near the back gates, she started her routine. In no time she was sweating. She took a refilled spa water bottle from her backpack.

As you read you can see different characters going to training. All three characters are the same (Jo) and are doing much the same thing. However, details make the second two come alive in your mind. Nothing much more is said about the girl's character but the detail gives an indication of her lifestyle.

EXERCISE A

(answer page 162)

Give specific examples (concrete detail) for these general terms. The first has been done for you.

suburb	Union, Kentucky	beach	____________	TV show	____________
tree	____________	sport	____________	flower	____________
juice	____________	magazine	____________	fruit	____________

Detail Gives Insight

Specific detail gives more than just facts. It gives an insight into the character or action. The idea works just as well for other parts of speech (adjectives, adverbs, verbs, and so on) as for nouns.

EXERCISE B

(answer page 162)

Which of the sentences below creates the best word picture?

1. Holding the chocolates behind his back, Mark went up to the door.
2. Hiding the wrapped box of chocolates behind his back, Mark stole up to the front door.

EXERCISE C

(answer page 162)

Rewrite these sentences using concrete detail. Think in terms of *what, how, who, when,* and *where.*

1. The dog sat in the mud. ____________________

____

____

2. Petra went into the cafe and placed her order. ____________________

____

____

3. Kelly lay on her bed and listened to the radio. ____________________

____

____

4. The parking lot had several vehicles waiting near a delivery dock. ____________________

____

____

Consistency

Make sure that the concrete detail is consistent with the character or setting. Below is a rewrite of the passage from page 22. Note how unrealistic some of the changes are.

> It was a stifling afternoon. Jo looked around the Olympic Sports Stadium for a place to prepare for her volleyball match. She didn't like being observed. Finding a far corner she removed her windbreaker and rolled down her socks. She always started with a few on-the-spot warm-up jogs before her stretches.
>
> Soon she was perspiring profusely. She rummaged in her school bag to find some left-over juice to quench her thirst.

Warning!

When in doubt about specific details, it is wise to use general terms rather than make mistakes.

EXERCISE D

(answer page 162)

Rewrite the following sentences using concrete detail. Each sentence may be expanded into more than one sentence.

1. The audience reacted to the musician's performance with admiration.

____

____

____

2. Insects were crawling all over the food set out for their meal.

____

____

____

3. She ate the cream-coated pie and washed it down with a drink.

____

____

____

4. The herd wandered over the dry land looking for food.

____

____

____

5. The sound of a military vehicle nearby sent people hurrying for cover.

____

____

____

6. A person stopped by the headstone and read the inscription.

____

____

____

EXERCISE E

Read this short extract and rewrite it (or part of it) adding concrete detail.

Write it with a particular type of person in mind: rich city worker; out-of-work, lazy or brash person; keen athlete; surfer. Keep the detail consistent with your selected character.

> Jake drove down the road towards the coast. He had the radio on and enjoyed his favorite music. Finally, as he turned off the road, he changed the radio for a tape.
>
> The road to the beach was little more than a track over rocky ground. Trees by the roadside often scraped the sides of his vehicle. Ruts in the road made the going slow.
>
> Releasing his seat belt, he took some food from a container on the passenger's seat.
>
> After several bites, he took a bottle from the container. The intense concentration was making him thirsty.
>
> Soon he would be at his destination. His home by the beach for a few days.

____

Briefly describe Jake's character in your rewrite. _______________________

____

6 Creating Evocative Opening Paragraphs

Paragraphs can be from one word long to several sentences long. The opening paragraph has to grab the reader's attention and make them want to find out more. Don't reveal too much. The opening paragraph should either **intrigue** the reader or **put questions** in the reader's mind: Who is this person? What is happening?

(answer page 163)

Read this opening paragraph and answer the question.

> The email was puzzling. No, it was confusing.
>
> I took it from the pocket of my denim jacket and reread the terrible typing. It was more than just the typing, it looked as if it had been written by someone not fully coherent, or as if it had been badly copied.
>
> From: *The Rats of Wolfe Island*

To what questions does the reader need answers? Here are two that may be raised in the reader's mind: Who is reading the email? Who wrote the email?

Write another question that needs an answer. ______________________________

____

To find the answers the reader will have to read on.

EXERCISE B

(answer page 163)

Read the opening paragraphs from the book *The Ghost Writer.*

> He came across the ad by accident. He didn't know why he was even looking at the pathetic magazine. They have the weirdest reading matter in some reception areas. Whoever was in charge put out anything they could lay their hands on. The magazines were more boring than the waiting. Some looked older than he was. They should all be trashed.
>
> Still, the ad was intriguing.

Write down three questions that may make a reader want to find out more.

1. ____

____

2. ____

____

3. ____

____

Writing Tip

Speech, especially starting in the middle of a conversation, can be a good beginning.

EXERCISE C

(answer page 163)

Read the passage and answer the questions.

"Can't you see it?" queried Matthew.

Arthur took a deep breath and then said, "Can't see a darn thing."

"Look to the right of the red object!" directed Matthew.

"You don't mean *that*?" growled Arthur, in disbelief.

What questions are already surfacing in your mind? Do you want to read on?

Write down two questions that may make a reader want to find out more.

1. ______________________________

2. ______________________________

Writing Tip

A striking first sentence with an unusual word or two can also be effective.

EXERCISE D

(answer page 163)

Read the short passage and answer the question.

The gargoyle stared down from the battlements with cold, granite eyes, onto the rabble in the cobblestone street below.

If you have used a really unusual word, you should give the reader some indication of what it means very soon in your story.

What material do you think a gargoyle is made from?

____

PLANTING QUESTIONS

Sometimes the writer will plant questions in the reader's mind. These questions may become part of the text. For example:

Sheryl crept into the front room. The Christmas tree was covered in flashing lights and presents were packed at its base. There was a big box to one side. What could be in it? Was it a present for her?

EXERCISE E

Look at some of your recent writing. Ask yourself these questions:

1. Is there too much information in the opening paragraph(s)? ______________________

____

2. Can some of the information be revealed later in the story? ______________________

____

3. Can any words be removed without destroying the meaning or sense? ______________________

____

4. How well does the opening relate to the rest of the story? ______________________

____

5. Does the opening make you want to read on and find out more? ______________________

____

EXERCISE F

(answer page 163)

Use a highlighter to strike out all the unnecessary words or phrases in this short passage so less information is revealed. (The first one is done for you.) Then, rewrite the passage on the lines below and on the next page.

Kon became aware that something **unexpected** was going to happen. Everyone was looking at something going on just behind his back. Looking right past his sandy hair to something not too far away. He wondered what it could be.

Slowly, he turned his sandy head.

Dee Song giggled at Fiona who was blowing a huge bubble.

Then there was an explosion, so loud and unexpected that he fell backwards off his bench seat onto the grass, his right hand taking the full force of his fall.

Then all the kids laughed loudly.

Kon struggled slowly to his feet and glared angrily at the small group and then he looked at his right hand and saw that he had chewing gum stuck to it.

Dee Song raised her hand to cover her mouth.

____

____

____

____

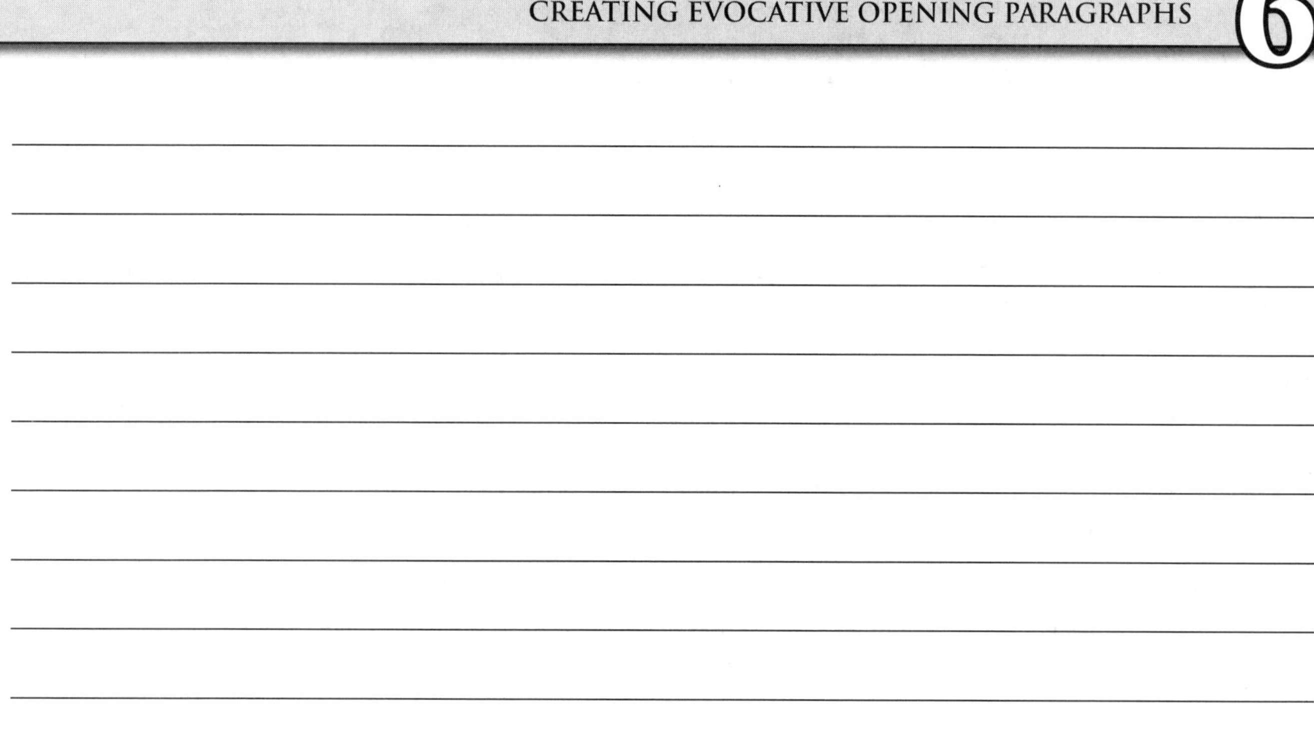

READING TASK

These are examples of paragraphs that arouse interest.

There was an eerie silence in the street as Joanne walked home from school. Puzzled, she looked around. Everything seemed normal. Some kids were chasing each other up ahead, and a truck rumbled noisily along the road. Just an ordinary afternoon, so why did everything seem stiller than usual?

From: "Zeppo" by Virginia King

Michael woke up with a start. Someone was banging on the front door. Heavy footsteps clomped over the bare boards of the hallway. A shouting of voices, Jacko's familiar growl, then the front door slammed shut. Michael shivered and pulled the thin blanket closer around his shoulders. Through the cracked glass of the curtainless window, the sky looked gray and dirty.

From: "Streetscape" by Ian Steep

Everyone in Dorking Street knew there was a spook in Gerry's attic wardrobe. Gerry told them all.

"Don't stay the night if you're scared of spooks," he would say the first time anyone came to stay. And the first time was always the last.

Gerry's house was the creepiest house in the street.

From: *Spooked* by Errol Broome

Writing Tip

The opening paragraph (or first few paragraphs) and the title are the first impressions the reader has of your story. They should catch the reader's attention.

7 Writing Closing Paragraphs

The closing paragraph(s) should tie up most of the important threads of your story. The reader should feel satisfied that the ordeals your character(s) has been through have been **resolved**. It doesn't always have to be a happy ending.

Rounding Off the Story

It is often a clever move to have the last few paragraphs reflect the first few paragraphs. This gives the story a rounded-off feeling.

In one of my recent books, which began with an email, this is the second to last paragraph.

> I touched the pocket of my denim jacket. The email that had brought me on this third and final trip was still there. It didn't take an Einstein to guess who–or what–had sent it.

From: *The Rats of Wolfe Island*

Exercise A

(answer page 163)

Read the opening and concluding paragraphs from these stories. Look for ways they tie the story up into a neat unit.

1. "Dream on, Brian"

Opening paragraphs:

> Some kids never learn.
>
> Take Brian for example. He was getting into deep water–in more ways than one. The small pod of whales was getting stressed as it moved through the tropical waters.

Closing paragraphs:

> . . . just sometimes, he [Brian] can be seen gazing into the cage thinking his canary just might be a little pterodactyl. Some kids never learn.
>
> Dream on, Brian.

List one way the author has tied the opening and closing paragraphs together.

---

2. *Bubble Buster*

Opening paragraphs:

> Buster loved pool parties. He could jump and bomb. He could splash and muck about. He jumped on Loren's blow-up seal. The seal burst. It hissed as it sped across the pool.
>
> "Wow," said Buster but Loren was not amused.

Closing paragraphs:

> Buster was falling. He thought he was going to break every bone in his body.
>
> "Splash!" He landed in the pool.
>
> As he got out of the water, Uncle Fred put a towel around his shoulders. Buster turned to his sister. "Thanks Loren. I owe you one."

List one way the author has tied the opening and closing paragraphs together.

____

EXERCISE B

(answer page 163)

In the second pair of paragraphs above (*Bubble Buster*), there is a change in attitude towards Loren.

How did Buster feel towards Loren in the opening paragraph? ______________________

____

____

How did Buster feel towards Loren in the closing paragraph? ______________________

____

____

EXERCISE C

(answer page 163)

Read the opening and closing paragraphs of *Holly and the Frog Prince* by Elaine Horsfield. The final paragraphs are almost a repeat of the opening paragraphs.

Opening paragraphs:

> Holly's mother read her a story about a princess that kissed a frog. The frog turned into a handsome prince, and they got married.
>
> "Revolting," said Holly, pulling a face. "You'd never catch me kissing a yukky frog."
>
> "I should hope not," said her mother kissing her goodnight.

Closing paragraphs:

> That night, she [Holly] hid the Frog Prince book under her bed.
>
> "Revolting," she said. "You won't catch me kissing a yukky frog."
>
> "I should hope not," said her mother as she turned out the light.

Write a phrase or sentence here that is almost a repeat of another phrase or sentence.

____

____

____

Writing Tip

If you write for young children, it is a good idea to include some repetition of sentences (or phrases) in your story. Very young children like the predictability. Many fairy tales use this technique (e.g., *The Three Little Pigs*).

EXERCISE D

(answer page 163)

Read this opening paragraph to a story titled "The Haunted Mine," and then write a concluding paragraph of two or three sentences.

> Jacinta walked down the dusty track towards the entrance of the old gold mine, then stopped. The broken sign warned, "Keep Out."
>
> She peered into the darkness. She could see nothing beyond the first few rotted and broken support beams. A bat suddenly swooped from nowhere into the black hole. She told herself there was nothing to be scared of. Still she hesitated.

____

____

____

____

____

____

____

____

RESEARCH

Reread the first and last few paragraphs of five books you have read recently and see how satisfactorily, in your opinion, the final paragraph(s) rounds off the story. Label them *unsatisfactory*, *satisfactory*, or *very satisfactory*, and give a brief explanation why.

Book	Opinion of First and Final Paragraph(s)
1. ____________	______________________________
2. ____________	______________________________
3. ____________	______________________________
4. ____________	______________________________
5. ____________	______________________________

ADDING CLOSING SENTENCES (CODAS)

A good concluding sentence doesn't necessarily add anything to the plot of your story, but it should give the reader a sense of the story being satisfactorily completed. It may add a little more insight into a character's new understanding of his or her self or world.

The final sentence may bring a smile to the reader's face, or a frown, or even shock the reader if it's a surprise ending.

Writing Tip

Unless you are very brave (or very foolish), don't use these concluding sentences:

"And they lived happily ever after."

"Then, I woke up and found it was all a dream."

EXERCISE A

(answer page 163)

Read the following conclusion of "Dream on, Brian." Highlight the last sentence.

> Brian looks after his canary very well, especially for someone who has had the most exciting experiences, but sometimes, just sometimes, he can be seen gazing into the cage thinking that the canary might just be a small pterodactyl.
>
> Some kids never learn.
>
> Dream on, Brian!

What does the last sentence really add to the story?

Not a lot, but it may bring a smile to the reader's face. The reader should feel that he or she has had a satisfactory read.

READING TASK

Read these concluding paragraphs, paying particular attention to the last sentences.

> "I think I'll go outside for a while," said Elmer to his mom. "I think I've had enough TV for one day!"
>
> "Are you okay?" asked his mother as she looked at him from the kitchen.
>
> "Yes," said Elmer. But he thought that there are some things that are really strange–so strange that they are hard to explain.

From: *The Strange Story of Elmer Floyd*

> I had won.
>
> I looked back at Claws. To my amazement, he smiled and gave me a tired "thumbs up" as I tumbled through the kids running onto the track to congratulate me.

From: *The Big Race*

ADDING CLOSING SENTENCES (CODAS)

In the conclusion to *The Big Race*, none of the information after "I had won" adds to the drama of the race. The race is over and the winner is known. The last sentence gives a sense of finality to the story. It doesn't leave it "hanging" and the reader feeling cheated.

RESEARCH

The final sentence (or two) of a story can be a **coda**, a term that is also used for the concluding passage of a piece of music. In story writing, a coda is a concluding part of the story that rounds it off, but is separate, from the main story.

Check three of your books or short stories for concluding sentences. Do some work better than others? Write the names of three stories you feel have effective codas and add the actual phrase or words that have been used. For example:

Jamie's a Hero by Susanne Gervay: "Yep, I'm glad we're home."

1. ____

____

2. ____

____

3. ____

____

EXERCISE B

(answer page 163)

Read these concluding paragraphs and highlight the codas (shown in italics).

> Sometimes I can see him [the skeleton] just inside the door [of the Ghost Train Ride] with his bony arms up in the air and his hands hanging down, scaring people. If he sees me, he waves and I wave back.
>
> *And sometimes Dad comes down to have a look, too!*

From: *My Sad Skeleton*

1. How does this coda make you, as a reader, feel? ______________

____

In the following story, everyone in town had their hair stolen but the mystery has been solved. Now read on.

> Santa Claus sneaked out and bought a big white wig and a pretend white beard while he waited for his real hair to grow, so he could go back into the shop and tell boys and girls what they might get for Christmas.
>
> *Do you know sometimes now he will wear a wig and pretend beard to remind himself of a time when he had no hair at all?*

From: *Great Hair Robbery*

2. How does this coda make you, as a reader, feel?

____

____

____

____

Writing Tip

The coda does not necessarily have to be a happy one.

EXERCISE C

(answer page 163)

Read the following extract and answer the question.

> They also tell me that the scars on the side of my face will look like laugh lines. They certainly don't look like laugh lines now and I can't see that they ever will, but that's what happens if you go round falling off motor bikes and letting them explode on you. The thumb has mended just fine.
>
> It should be Happy Ever After time at the Quinns' house, I suppose, but life isn't as easy as that. I keep seeing Dodie propped up on fancy cushions in Mrs. McKibbon's front kitchen.
>
> *I'll never forget the dead look on her face.*
>
> From: *The Kidnapping of Susie Q* by Catherine Sefton

How would you describe the ending? _______________

____

____

____

____

EXERCISE D

(answer page 163)

Write an amusing, original final sentence for these four popular tales. For example:
Jack and the Beanstalk: Jack decided there and then never, ever to eat beans.

1. *Three Little Pigs*: _______________

____

____

____

2. A Batman and Robin adventure: ______________________________

3. *Goldilocks and the Three Bears*: ______________________________

4. *The Hare and the Tortoise*: ______________________________

5. A book of your choice. Title: ______________________________

EXERCISE E

(answer page 163)

Write a serious, original final sentence for this conclusion. The narrator is attending the funeral of his Auntie Dawn but is not totally satisfied with the ceremony. Now read on.

> They didn't bury Auntie Dawn in the village where she spent the last years of her life. They buried her in the town where she married Uncle Dan. She hadn't been back there since 1963. That was the year Uncle Dan left for "services overseas."
>
> I stood back and watched the mourners by the grave. I only half listened to the words of the country minister. He had never met Auntie Dawn. I wondered how genuine his words could be. I wondered *what* he could be thinking.

Revision

There are four main sentence types, all of which can be used in fiction writing.

Sentence type	Example
1. Statement	Ms. Lee has a blue station wagon.
2. Question	Where did you leave my car keys?
3. Exclamation	Good grief, it's getting closer!
4. Command	Come here at once.

Exercise A

(answer page 164)

Name these sentence types:

1. A red sky at night warns farmers of hot weather to come. ____________________
2. I've been bitten! ____________________
3. Pass your book to the teacher, Graham. ____________________
4. Take your elbows off the table. ____________________
5. Where did you find a shirt that color? ____________________

Incomplete sentences

Writers often use incomplete sentences for effect. They may use just a word or two or a phrase, or even start with *and*. Incomplete sentences are acceptable in narratives but less acceptable in most other writing.

Writing Tip

Remember to use a variety of sentence types in your story (and not only in direct speech). One or two exclamations or questions every so often can improve your writing.

EXERCISE B

(answer page 164)

Read this passage and look for several different sentence types.

> I don't know what caused the accident. Could it have been the wet road? Most likely someone had been tampering with the brakes on my bicycle. Sudsy! That was the first name to come to my mind. He was called Sudsy because he was Cold Power, like the washing powder. No one called him Sudsy to his face. Not until now!
>
> Just thinking that was my first mistake.

How many exclamations were used? ______________________

EXERCISE C

(answer page 164)

Add the correct punctuation to this extract to show which sentences are statements, questions, commands, and exclamations. (Some of the sentences can be punctuated in different ways, depending on how they are used.)

> It works, it really works__ I can hardly believe it__ My invention is working__ It has been running for more than three minutes and is still working__ Scientists from all over the world will want to see it__ They will be speechless__ Newspaper reporters will come with their photographers to do feature articles on me__ And what will I tell them__ I will say this is the first fully automatic short story writer__

EXERCISE D

Write a paragraph or two using at least two sentence types. A title has been provided. (For this exercise don't quote any speech in your writing.)

The First Ride on a Roller Coaster

____

____

____

____

____

____

____

____

____

____

____

EXERCISE E

(answer page 164)

Read this extract from *Sit Down, Mom, There's Something I've Got to Tell You* by Moya Simons. It is made interesting by using different sentence types. Then, answer the questions.

> Saturday morning. School holidays. Mom is sitting at the breakfast table in her spotted PJs. I am sitting opposite watching a beetle scurrying towards the sugar bowl. Life is full of uncertainty. Do I kill it—thereby wiping out generation after generation of future beetles? I mean, who knows? One might be a special beetle destined to lead insects out of the dark age into the brave new world of tomorrow.
>
> While I think about this, Mom suddenly says, "Sometimes I get lonely."

1. The extract starts with two incomplete sentences. They are used to grab the reader's attention. How could the two incomplete sentences be combined to make one proper sentence?

____

____

2. Excluding incomplete sentences, how many sentence types have been used?

____

____

The character who is telling the story in the story is called the <u>narrator</u>. The person who wrote the story is called the <u>author</u>.

The author, Paul Jennings, wrote a book called *The Gizmo*. The story is told by Stephen Wilkins, the main character. He is the narrator.

Writing Tip

The use of question sentences puts the reader in the narrator's mind to share his or her feelings and thoughts.

EXERCISE F

(answer page 164)

Read this passage, which makes use of question-type sentences. Then answer the questions on the next page.

> The explorer came to a small stream flowing over some sharp, bare rocks. How far had he hiked? He didn't know. How much time had he wasted taking the wrong direction? He didn't know. How long would his boots last under such conditions? He didn't know. Oddly, he didn't care anymore.
>
> With bent back and aching legs he stood at the water's edge, almost too afraid to bend down to drink.

1. How many of his own questions has the narrator answered? ______________________

2. What feature do you notice about the answers? ______________________

____

3. What effect does this have? ______________________

____

____

____

EXERCISE G

(answer page 164)

1. Highlight the incomplete sentences in this passage.

   The tire tracks led to the top of the last red sand dune. Below, the gibber desert stretched to a lost horizon. No one could survive out there.

   The car must have rolled. Over and over. There was a succession of scars in the sand right down the steep side of the dune. These were slowly disappearing, as the endlessly moving sand smothered all evidence of human intrusion. Where were the occupants now? Entombed under tons of sand.

   The battered car stood awkwardly on its wheels at the base of the dune.

2. Highlight the word that best describes the feelings created by the incomplete sentence.

   despair   restlessness   bitterness   relief

RESEARCH

Find books in your library and list them below. See how the authors have used a variety of sentence types to draw the reader into their stories.

____

____

____

____

____

____

____

____

____

____

____

The rhetorical question is a device that fiction writers can incorporate into their writing to hold the attention of the reader. Rhetorical questions are questions to which **no answer is expected**. We use them all the time in our everyday conversations (e.g., Why didn't I think of that?).

Writing Tip

By using rhetorical questions, the writer can put the reader into the character's mind and share his or her experiences and emotions.

EXERCISE A

(answer page 164)

Read this extract from the story "Harley." The incident occurs at the end of Harley's first day at school. Highlight the two rhetorical questions and complete the exercise below.

> At the end of Harley's first school day, his parents waited anxiously in the school grounds.
>
> Harley's new class came out, smiling and laughing.
>
> Where was Harley? Where was his teacher?
>
> "Oh my," whispered Harley's mom, "I don't like this."
>
> His dad remained silent for a moment before saying, "Look, there's his teacher!"

Give two words that may describe the parents' feelings.

______________________, ______________________

EXERCISE B

(answer page 164)

Read the extract from *Sit Down, Mom, There's Something I've Got to Tell You* by Moya Simons. Highlight the rhetorical questions and complete the exercise below.

> Saturday morning. School holidays. Mom is sitting at the breakfast table in her spotted PJs. I am sitting opposite watching a beetle scurrying towards the sugar bowl. Life is full of uncertainty. Do I kill it–thereby wiping out generation after generation of future beetles? I mean, who knows? One might be a special beetle destined to lead insects out of the dark age into the brave new world of tomorrow.
>
> While I think about this, Mom suddenly says, "Sometimes I get lonely."

Give two words that may describe the narrator's feelings.

______________________, ______________________

EXERCISE C

(answer page 164)

Read the following passage and highlight the rhetorical questions.

> Someone must have prepared the report. Was it a scientist? Was it a journalist? The first thing anyone knew was from a television report. The report was aired just after the 10 o'clock news on a Tuesday. Who watches television that time of night?
>
> By 10 o'clock the next morning everyone was talking about it. An iceberg had drifted right up to the Victorian coast. There it stopped without an explanation from anyone. Maybe it was a plastic hoax. Or was it something more sinister? Had the polar icecaps begun to melt?

Give two words that may describe the narrator's feelings. ____________, ____________

EXERCISE D

(answer page 164)

Read the following extracts and add your own rhetorical question on the line provided.

1. Matthew struggled up the steep incline. It was not vertical but close enough, with just enough rocks to find a new foothold or handhold every meter or so. He had been climbing for over an hour, and the rocks were warming in the early morning sun. Exhaustion was becoming a problem. Height was another problem, and he didn't know how far he had climbed. Or how far he had to go.

   ____

2. Sheryl crept into the front room. The Christmas tree was covered in flashing lights and presents were packed at its base.

   There were a number of small but fancy presents at the front of the tree. There was a big box to one side.

   ____

EXERCISE E

(answer page 164)

In the following extract from "Zeppo," Virginia King has used a rhetorical question which shows the narrator's concern and puzzlement.

> There was an eerie silence in the street as Joanne walked home from school. Puzzled, she looked around. Everything seemed normal. Some kids were chasing each other up ahead, and a truck rumbled noisily along the road. Just an ordinary afternoon, <u>so why did everything seem stiller than usual?</u>

Suggest an alternative rhetorical question that shows another feeling, such as fear or amusement.

____

EXERCISE F

Get a copy of *The Iron Man* by Ted Huges or choose another book and find some passages that make use of rhetorical questions.

The length of sentences in your story writing can have a positive effect on the quality of your writing. Sentence lengths are important for **special effects** in your story, as well as for maintaining reader interest and excitement.

EXERCISE A

(answer page 164)

Read this "poorly" written passage and compare it with the following passage that makes use of sentences of different lengths.

Passage 1

Pablo hurried to the door of the quiet hut. He kept his back bent and head down. At the door he removed his gloves. Then, he gently tapped the wooden door. No sound came from inside the hut. Pablo gently turned the metal door handle. Holding the handle, he pushed the door firmly. The door swung open quietly. Pablo quickly stepped back against the wall.

Passage 2

With his head down and back bent, Pablo hurried to the door of the quiet hut. After removing his gloves, he tapped gently on the wooden door. Silence. Not a sound from inside. Gently, he turned the metal door handle and pushed. The door glided open. Pablo quickly stepped back against the wall.

Which passage creates the most tension and suspense? ______________________________

Explain your choice. ______________________________

____

SHORT SENTENCES

Short sentences are usually best for exciting or tense moments in your stories. Longer sentences tend to suit descriptions.

Read this extract as an example of short sentences used to create a sense of pain.

He was on his knees. They held. His back held, stiff. If I'm asked what happened to me, I'll say . . . "It's a long story!" In agony, painfully slow, grunting, Andres sets his engines going. He whips himself with words, blast you–heave! Gallop you lazy horse. He was up, dizzy, swaying, tall as El Plomo, capped with eternal snow.

He moved. One pace. One for Juan. Stop, sway. Another pace. One for Horatio. One for Braulio. One for Don. And for Isa. Ah! He sucked in his breath. He stumbled forward across the shingle onto the gray-white stones, the sky above him swinging like a boat in a storm.

From: *Talking in Whispers* by James Watson

EXERCISE B

(answer page 164)

Rewrite these short sentences as one long sentence. You may have to use conjunctions (joining words such as *and, but, because*) and commas.

1. Craig found his pen. He had to find his book. It was not in his bag.

2. Behind the seat Nettie saw a bus ticket. Near the ticket was a coin. The coin was a ten-cent coin.

3. It was a tropical tree. The tree was covered in long slender leaves. Among the leaves was a sprinkling of blue flowers. There was a carpet of flowers on the ground.

EXERCISE C

(answer page 164)

Rewrite these long sentences as short sentences.

1. The clown dove through the flaming hoop to finish with a forward roll but the curled toe of his shoe caught the hoop and suddenly his costume was on fire.

2. The castle was dark and Kate felt very frightened as she peered into the gloom and chains started to rattle at the bottom of the stone stairs.

3. On the island there are several types of vehicles, including a small truck for picking up cargo, several beat-up taxis for the stray tourists, and a noisy mini-bus.

RESEARCH

Look through some novels and see if you can find some single-word sentences or even single-word paragraphs. Write some of the words you find here.

____

____

____

____

Examine the situations in which the words were used (e.g., war action, suspense, excitement, horror, comedy, sports action).

Writing Tip

Smart writers will combine the skills learned in Chapter 9 "Using Different Sentence Types" with those developed from working this chapter.

EXERCISE D

(answer page 164)

Rewrite this passage using a variety of sentence lengths. You may have to change the text to get the result you want.

> Chrissy twirled the string bag round and round her extended hand as she headed towards the supermarket. As it was Friday afternoon, she was looking forward to a long weekend with her friend Tracey Goodman. They had planned many exciting activities, such as watching the late night horror movie, eating pizza in her bedroom, playing Tracey's latest CDs, and talking privately.
>
> The afternoon sun was low in the western sky and the wide main street of Brookville offered little protection from its warm rays, but she didn't mind.

____

____

____

____

____

____

____

____

____

____

Recommendations

Here are just a few books that use sentence lengths effectively. There are many others. Check out some other books in your school or class library. There is space for you to add to the list.

The John Marsden trilogy

James Watson, *Talking in Whispers*

E.B. White, *Charlotte's Web*

Paul Jennings, *The Cabbage Patch Fib*

Morris Gleitzman, *Two Weeks with the Queen*

Parts of Speech

Here is a quick review of parts of speech.

→ **Nouns** are naming words (e.g., *cow, crowd, annoyance*).

→ **Pronouns** are words used instead of a noun (e.g., *I, him, her, she, it, them, your*).

→ **Prepositions** often refer to the position of things (e.g., *on, above, beside, past*).

→ **Verbs** include thinking, doing, and saying words, as well as being and having ones (e.g., *run, running, wonder, shouted, is, had, polished*).

→ **Adjectives** are describing words that add meaning to a noun (e.g., *red, two, cold, sweet, biggest, best, unhappy*).

→ **Adverbs** tell how, when, where, or why something happened (e.g., *slowly, soon, here, during, sometimes*).

→ **Conjunctions** are joining words (e.g., *and, but, because, yet, or*).

Beginning Sentences

Any of these types of words can be used as sentence beginnings. They will add sparkle and interest to your story writing.

Dead trees lined the banks of the dry stream. (adjective)

Along the banks of the dry stream were lines of dead trees. (preposition)

Lining the banks of the dry stream were dead trees. (verb)

Exercise A

(answer page 165)

Rewrite the sentence below using two different sentence beginnings. (You may have to make a few changes.)

Fences won't stop red foxes in their silent hunt for prey.

1. ______________________________

____

2. ______________________________

____

EXERCISE B

(answer page 165)

Write your own sentences starting with the words given.

1. All ____________________
2. Buzzing ____________________
3. Before ____________________
4. Tuesdays ____________________

EXERCISE C

(answer page 165)

Read this extract and highlight the words that have been used as sentence beginnings.

> Large drops of water began to thud onto the verandah and rattle across the iron roof of the [vacation] cottage. Aaron guessed it was a tropical squall coming in from the ocean, drenching the small outer islands of the lagoon as it came.
>
> Suddenly, there was a flash of lightning followed by a clap of thunder, just above the cottage. Then the skies opened up and the rain poured down.
>
> Aaron could just hear his father stumbling around in the next room closing the windows. But no light came on.

From: *Aitutaki Phantom*

What parts of speech are the beginning words?

Large: ____________ Aaron: ____________ Suddenly: ____________

Then: ____________ But: ____________

EXERCISE D

(answer page 165)

Here is a "poorly" written extract.

> The sun was just coming up over a moon crater. The time was one o'clock back in Sydney. The captain of the spacecraft put on his space suit. The task was slow, but finally he was fully suited for a moonwalk. The engineer gave his chief a quick wink as the airlock door opened. The captain entered the airlock and the door hissed closed. The captain was now on his own. He tried the outer door of the airlock. The door didn't move.

1. Which word has been overused as a sentence beginning? ____________________

2. Rewrite the extract using a number of different sentence beginnings, but keep the general meaning.

Writing Tip

Too many unusual word beginnings can be off-putting to the reader. It's okay to use *the, a, then, she,* and so on, just remember to vary your sentence beginnings.

EXERCISE E

(answer page 165)

Rewrite these sentences in a more interesting way–start with different words.

1. Morris had to wait in the bus shelter so he found a crossword to complete.

2. Many helpers in the kitchen will create chaos.

3. Fred was the youngest and he had to have first go on the swing.

____

____

____

4. Andy used his knowledge and his common sense to repair the mower.

____

____

____

Writing Tip

Occasionally you can start an incomplete sentence with a conjunction. It can add impact to your writing (e.g., "And that's just what she did!")–but don't overdo it.

EXERCISE F

(answer page 165)

Read this extract from *Talking in Whispers* by James Watson, and then complete the exercise below.

> There had been no celebrations, no treats for Andres Larreta, and no treatment for his injuries. Dumped, rib broke; maybe more than one. Eyes swollen, flesh to the bone; blood in trickles from his hair and his nose. Groin afire with pain.
>
> Half-conscious, mouthing words yet inaudible. Words of terror, of nightmare. Slung into the wet. Lying, strings loose.
>
> Tough guy?
>
> Andres the puppet, performance ended, fallen from his one-wheel bicycle, without applause. No songs. No more songs. No arms strong enough, no fingers unlocked enough to strum the charango. Blue lightning and white. And finally black.

1. What does the last sentence suggest to you, the reader? ______________________

____

____

____

2. Give two adjectives used as sentence beginnings.

______________________, ______________________

3. Give two nouns used as sentence beginnings.

______________________, ______________________

Repetition is another technique of a competent writer, but like most techniques you can have too much of a good thing. Repetition must have purpose.

REPETITION OF A WORD

Words can be repeated for **emphasis**. How does repetition strengthen the meaning? Look at the following sentences and highlight the repeated words.

The noise from the new band was very, very loud.

Mice, mice, and more mice scampered from the shed when the fire started.

He was tired, so tired that as soon as he settled on the bus seat he went to sleep.

EXERCISE A

(answer page 165)

Write two of your own sentences repeating the words *people* and *wind.*

(people) ______________________________

(wind) ______________________________

REPETITION OF A SENTENCE

Repeating a sentence **stresses the point**. Many fairy tales make use of a repeated sentence. Two that come to mind are *The Three Little Pigs* (I'll huff and I'll puff . . .) and *Goldilocks* (descriptions of chairs and so on). They add a sense of rhythm to the tale.

In a story for younger readers, *Maria's Coin*, the sentence "Once Maria decided to do something, she did it" is repeated several times throughout the story. This not only provides some rhythm to the story but emphasizes the determination of the main character, Maria.

REPETITION VARIATIONS

Varying the sentence or phrase can reinforce an idea, but it can also advance your story. Look at these examples.

Entering the bank was a puzzled guard. Leaving the bank was a calm actress.

Maria had black hair, black eyes, wore black clothes, but she still looked as if she were going to have a fun time.

EXERCISE B

(answer page 165)

Reread these sentences from *Talking in Whispers* by James Watson. Andres is the narrator.

> He moved. One pace. One for Juan. Stop, sway. Another pace. One for Horatio. One for Braulio. One for Don. And for Isa. Ah! He sucked in his breath. He stumbled forward across the shingle onto the gray-white stones, the sky above him swinging like a boat in a storm.

1. What phrase is most often repeated, with variations? ______________________________

2. What does this tell you about the attitude of Andres? ______________________________

____

EXERCISE C

Select four books for younger readers and find an example of repetition in each.

Book/Story	Repeated Words/Phrases/Sentences
____________________	______________________________
____________________	______________________________
____________________	______________________________
____________________	______________________________

EXERCISE D

(answer page 165)

Read this extract from "Cow Dung Custard," from *Unreal!* by Paul Jennings.

> Flies, flies, flies. They hung around the house all day and all night. It was the smell of the manure. The smell attracted them. There were flies everywhere; they came down the chimney and under the doors. People had no trouble finding our house. If anyone asked where we lived, they were always told the same thing. "Just stop at the house with the flies."

1. You will have noticed that the word *flies* is not only repeated in the first sentence, but is mentioned several times later in that paragraph. Briefly describe the effect the multiple use of the words *flies* has upon you as a reader.

____

____

____

____

2. What is the effect of the repetition of the word *all* in the second sentence ("all day and all night")? The sentence, "They hung around the house all the time," has almost the same meaning but was not used.

EXERCISE E

Write your own short paragraph repeating the word *rain*. You might like to model your paragraph on the above paragraph by Paul Jennings.

EXERCISE F

(answer page 165)

Highlight a word that could be repeated to give these sentences more impact.

> There was mud everywhere. Thick, black, sticky mud. It was on my jogging suit. There was even some in my shorts and underpants. There were globs of it in my ears and in my hair.

1. What word did you highlight? ______

2. Rewrite the passage making use of the repetition of that word.

Repetition of a Sound

Repetition of a sound is called **alliteration** (e.g., rolling rocks). This helps to create atmosphere in your writing. It is often used effectively in poetry. It does not have to be the sound that starts the word. For example:

Slowly and silently the silver stars sailed across the sea of space.

The repetition of the "s" sound is meant to create a feeling of peace and tranquillity. Consider the different effect when the sentence is rewritten like this:

Twinkling stars roamed the outer reaches of the black universe.

EXERCISE G

(answer page 165)

Write a sentence about bugles using alliteration.

____

____

____

EXERCISE H

(answer page 165)

Read this extract, looking for repetition of a particular sound (not word).

Three large tiger sharks were circling closer and closer. Brian could see the glint in their mean menacing eyes, and their rows of triangular teeth as they swam nearer and nearer their defenseless victims. Brian knew they were tiger sharks because they were fierce and dangerous.

From: "Dream on, Brian"

1. Write two words that repeat your selected sound.

______________________, ______________________

2. What feeling does the sound help to create for you?

____

____

____

3. Suggest an alliterative adjective for tiger.

____

____

____

For their stories many students rely heavily on what is seen. This is important, as sight is one of our most important senses when developing a story. However, it is not the only sense with which we can take in information.

EXERCISE A

(answer page 165)

What are the other four senses?

__________, __________, __________, __________

EXERCISE B

(answer page 166)

Read the following paragraph and work out the sense the author has used.

> William's old car scrunched to a stop in the gravel near the gate. The motor gave a couple of sickly coughs before it died. As William pushed the driver's door open, the rusting hinges gave a metal groan. Freeing himself from the car, William stretched and yawned loudly and slammed the door shut. Somewhere beneath the chassis a loose exhaust pipe rattled.

What sense does the author mostly rely on for his description? __________

EXERCISE C

1. Look at a piece of your recent writing and list the senses you have incorporated into your work.

____

____

____

____

2. Which sense did you rely on most? __________
3. Can you see ways of including reference to other senses? __________

____

____

____

EXERCISE D

(answer page 166)

Read the passage on page 56 and see how many different senses the author has used.

USING ALL THE SENSES—INTRODUCTION/WHAT DO YOU SEE?

William walked to the neat, white gate over loose, coarse gravel. He lifted the cold latch and hesitated. A rather odd sound came from behind the garage next to the brick cottage. He peered down the drive but saw nothing. He pushed the gate open. It swung freely until it hit, with a clunk, a metal peg that protruded from the ground by the drive. It was evidently meant to protect the fragrant rosebush from being battered by any careless opening of the gate. Suddenly, he got a whiff of burning rubber.

What senses has the writer used?

__________, __________, __________, __________

EXERCISE E

(answer page 166)

Look at these brief descriptions of water and note the use of different senses:

sparkling water, salty water, stagnant water, chilly water, gurgling water

Describe *stones, rain,* and *truck* using several different senses.

__________ stones, __________ stones, __________ stones, __________ stones

__________ rain, __________ rain, __________ rain, __________ rain, __________ rain

__________ truck, __________ truck, __________ truck, __________ truck

Writing Tip

Adjectives are effective words for incorporating the senses into your writing. They are often called describing words as they add meaning to nouns.

EXERCISE F

(answer page 166)

Look at the underlined adjectives in this sentence and write down how they have added meaning to the nouns.

<u>Two</u> <u>hungry</u> dogs sat on the <u>damp</u> grass by the <u>back</u> door of the <u>abandoned</u> shed.

1. Two hungry dogs: ____________________

2. damp grass: ____________________

3. back door: ____________________

4. abandoned shed: ____________________

EXERCISE G

(answer page 166)

1. Add adjectives in the spaces to give this short passage more "sense" appeal.

Val caught a glimpse of the __________ van through the __________ crowd. It was by a __________ tree near a __________ bus stop where some __________ locals squatted around a __________ fire. __________ smoke curled up from a __________ drum.

2. What senses were you able to include in your selection of adjectives?

____

EXERCISE H

(answer page 166)

In the space write the sense the adjective is portraying when describing the noun. The first is done for you.

chirping birds	hearing	scented envelope	__________
hot motor	__________	jangling chains	__________
dazzling sun	__________	salty chips	__________
sweet coffee	__________	dry paint	__________

EXERCISE I

(answer page 166)

Rewrite the following passage, replacing the underlined "sense" adjectives with adjectives referring to another sense. Notice the effect it has on the writing.

> A cold wind whipped through the dead leaves of the thin poplars and across the rutted street. A tired policeman standing on a deserted corner caught a whiff of decaying garbage. Taking a crumpled tissue from his sagging pocket, he covered his tingling nose.

____

____

____

____

____

____

____

____

____

EXERCISE J

(answer page 166)

Change the "feel"-type adjectives to "sight"-type adjectives in this sentence:

It was a cold morning when Jim found a wet shirt on a spiky thornbush.

It was a ___________ morning when Jim found a ___________ shirt on a ___________ thornbush.

EXERCISE K

(answer page 166)

Sight is one of our most treasured senses. In this extract from *Charlotte's Web*, E.B. White has made clever use of her observations. Highlight four observations you find impressive.

> The next day was foggy. Everything on the farm was dripping wet. The grass looked like a magic carpet. The asparagus patch looked like a silver forest.
>
> On foggy mornings, Charlotte's web was truly a thing of beauty. This morning each tiny strand was decorated with tiny beads of water. The web glistened in the light, and made a pattern of loveliness and mystery, like a delicate veil. Even Lurvy, who wasn't particularly interested in beauty, noticed the web when he came with the pig's breakfast. He noted how clearly it showed up and noted how big and carefully built it was. And then he took another look and he saw something that made him set the pails down.

Writing Tip

See Chapter 26 for help and exercises on the better use of *look/see* words in your writing.

Using the sense of **touch** can add impact to your story. (In this chapter *feel* refers to physical touch, not to the emotions.) When you describe how something feels, the reader may be able to bring his or her own understanding to your work.

Look at these sentences: Sue pushed her foot into the boot. She felt something soft!

Soft could raise several questions in the reader's mind. Was it a sock? Was it a frog?

(answer page 166)

Read this passage and note how the author has made use of the sense of feeling. Highlight the words that you think refer to feeling or touching something.

> Fiona made her way across the bare, damp boards of the chilly room. Patches of the floor were so smooth that once or twice she almost slipped. In spots there were dark, sticky stains, as if oil had partially dried on the floor. Finally, she reached the window. With her finger, she rubbed a lop-sided circle in the coating of frost and grime that covered the entire surface. Then, before putting her finger in her warm mouth, she rubbed it clean on the coarse fabric of her coat.

Writing Tip

Remember, we don't feel only with our hands and fingers. Our whole body is a feeling machine.

"Feeling" words

Here are some of the things we might feel: *size, heat/cold, aches, glare, pressure, wet/dry, hard/soft, rough/smooth, oily, slimy.*

Feeling isn't one extreme or the other. Something doesn't have to be hot or cold. There are a lot of words that may go in between these two extremes.

Look at the range of words between the extremes of *agonizing* and *pleasant.*

←——————————————————→

agonizing, painful, aching, hurting, sore, tender, soothing, **pleasant**

It's these in-between words that are often more useful and descriptive.

EXERCISE B

(answer page 166)

Fill in your own in-between words for these examples:

1. wet ______________________________ dry
2. hot ______________________________ cold
3. hard ______________________________ soft
4. rough ______________________________ silky

Writing Tip

Keep a list of "feel" words you might like to use or can substitute for words commonly used when writing about things we feel.

EXERCISE C

(answer page 166)

1. Add to this list any "feel"-type words you find that are expressive or unusual.

   rigid, tingling, unevenness, sharp, heavy, numb, brittle, breathless, choking, vertigo

   ________ ________ ________ ________ ________ ________

2. Keep a list of some of the unusual or odd feelings you have had, and what caused them. You might be able to use these in your story writing. An example has been done for you.

Feeling	Cause
the itch	from an insect bite

EXERCISE D

(answer page 166)

Use your thesaurus to find two or three synonyms (words with similar meanings) for these "feel" words.

flexible ______ ______ ______

throbbing ______ ______ ______

tepid ______ ______ ______

jar ______ ______ ______

EXERCISE E

(answer page 166)

Use your dictionary to find the meaning for these "feel" words.

harrowing ______

smart ______

stun ______

numb ______

tingle ______

feverish ______

EXERCISE F

Find five other "feeling" words and give the dictionary meaning for them.

1. ______: ______
2. ______: ______
3. ______: ______
4. ______: ______
5. ______: ______

EXERCISE G

(answer page 166)

Read this passage and highlight all the "feeling" words or phrases.

The truck jerked gently as Dan changed up a gear. The open flat road lay before him. The huge engine gently ticking over produced a soft rhythm of sound and pleasant throbbing vibrations. The cabin was warm, and the steering wheel comfortable to hold. He could have been in a giant cocoon or, better still, the cockpit of a jumbo jet. The ride was that smooth.

The road beneath his wheels hummed monotonously and even the occasional dip or road repair gave little more than a kindly lift. It was like a gentle pat on the buttocks.

Dan checked his gauges. No problems there. He tapped the fuel indicator. The needle flickered for a moment, then became stationary. All was well.

Time for a bit of music, he thought, and pressed the start button on the CD player.

EXERCISE H

(answer page 167)

List some of the "feeling" words or phrases that you think of when looking at these characters.

1.

____

____

____

____

____

____

____

____

2.

____

____

____

____

____

____

____

____

____

Using All the Senses—What Do You Hear? 16

Using the sense of hearing can add quite dramatically to your story. In horror stories, it can be very effective (though it is often overdone!).

Exercise A

(answer page 167)

Read the passage and note how the author has made use of the sense of hearing. Highlight the "hearing" words.

> When the laughter of the other campers finally ceased, Ken expected silence. He longed for silence. But instead of silence, the wilderness outside was full of strange sounds.
>
> A bird's mournful cry could be heard in a nearby, whispering tree. The monotonous trickle of the creek was like the incessant arguing of a distant group of children. Then he isolated the buzzing and hissing of strange insects, the rustling in the dry grass just by the tent where he was to sleep. He even became aware of his own breathing.

Exercise B

(answer page 167)

Here is a list of nouns that can be used to describe types of sounds instead of words more commonly used. Add some more words to the list.

echo, uproar, rattle, scrape, report, bubble, hiss, clang, blare, racket, commotion

__________ __________ __________ __________ __________ __________

Writing Tip

Sometimes it is a good idea to put the actual sound in your story. **Onomatopoeia** refers to words that imitate the actual sound they are describing (e.g., clip-clop, fizz, oompah).

Exercise C

(answer page 167)

1. Highlight the examples of onomatopoeia used in this passage.

> Jim lay in his bed, waiting. Every so often someone clumped down the hallway–clomp, clomp, clomp. He listened until he could no longer hear the footsteps. Then the wooden staircase creaked. Someone was coming noiselessly. He hoped he had been forgiven–and forgotten. He began to relax.
>
> Rat-a-tat-tat!
>
> The knock on his door was so loud, so demanding, that he gasped and sat up with a start.
>
> "You can't come in," he cried in a squeaky voice.

2. Add to this list of "sound" words: *clang, whoosh, tick-tock*

______ ______ ______ ______ ______ ______

EXERCISE D

(answer page 167)

Keep a list of some of the unusual or odd sounds you have heard, and where you heard them. You might be able to use them in your story writing. One has been done for you.

Sound	Place
the squelch	of a boot being pulled out of mud
______	______
______	______
______	______
______	______

"HEARING" WORDS

Hearing sounds aren't one thing or the other. Sounds don't have to be melodious or jarring to the ear. There are many words that may go in between these two extremes.

Look at the range of words between the extremes of *deafening* and *silent*.

deafening, blaring, noisy, loud, distracting, audible, soft, faint, **silent**

←――――――――――――――――→

It's the in-between words that are often more useful and descriptive.

EXERCISE E

(answer page 167)

Fill in some in-between words for these examples:

cheep ______________________ screech

thunderclap ______________________ snap

EXERCISE F

(answer page 167)

Learn the actual names of the sounds animals make. What animals make these sounds?

hiss ______________, yowl ______________, warble ______________, mew ______________

honk ______________, trumpet ______________, bleat ______________, grunt ______________

EXERCISE G

(answer page 167)

Use your thesaurus to find two or three synonyms (words with similar meanings) for these "sound" words.

whimper ______________ ______________ ______________

tuneful ______________ ______________ ______________

rowdy ______________ ______________ ______________

titter ______________ ______________ ______________

rant ______________ ______________ ______________

claptrap ______________ ______________ ______________

EXERCISE H

(answer page 167)

1. Use your dictionary to find the meaning for these "sound" words.

cacophony ______________________________

tattoo ______________________________

bass ______________________________

yelp ______________________________

bay ______________________________

catcall ______________________________

2. What is being talked about if someone uses the word *tintinnabulation*? __________

EXERCISE I

Find five other "sound" words and give the dictionary meaning for them.

1. ______________: ____

2. ______________: ____

3. ______________: ____

4. ______________: ____

5. ______________: ____

EXERCISE J

(answer page 167)

Read this passage and highlight all the "sound"-type words or phrases.

> Down in the darkened bedroom Penelope was peeping out of the bedclothes with Fred, listening to the tap, tap tapping as the Googyman's cane came closer and closer to the windowsill.
>
> A storm was building up. Perfect Googyman condition, Fred had whispered. Just the weather he needs to finish zapping the window locks.
>
> Tap, tap, tap. Penelope looked across at Fred's trembling head on the other side of the elephant skin boot. Tap, tap, tap, tap, tap, tap, tap, tap, tap!
>
> A roll of thunder followed a crack of lightning across the house and almost through the room.

From: *Freddie the Frightened* by Pamela Shrapnel

EXERCISE K

(answer page 167)

List some of the "hearing" words or phrases that you associate with cooking.

____________________ ____________________

____________________ ____________________

____________________ ____________________

____________________ ____________________

____________________ ____________________

____________________ ____________________

____________________ ____________________

Using all the senses—What do you smell?

Using the sense of smell can add to the atmosphere of your story. Describing how something smells may allow the reader to bring his or her own understanding to your work, as well as evoking a strong mental image in the reader's mind.

(answer page 167)

Compare these sentences, and place a checkmark by the one you think has the greater impact.

1. Julie caught a whiff of food cooking. Spicy sausages, or some sort of meat.
2. Julie smelled food cooking. It might be sausages, or some sort of meat.

Briefly explain your choice. ____

____

EXERCISE B

(answer page 168)

Read this passage and note how the author has made use of the sense of smell. Highlight the words that refer to "smelling."

> Randy sniffed once. Then he sniffed again. He looked around the bus shelter, nose held high like a hound trying to identify the origin of a scent. The fumes from the departed bus were upsetting but there was something else. It wasn't a foul smell. It was a pleasant aroma. It had the trace of a sharp perfume or scent that seemed to sting the inside of his nostrils.

Writing Tip

Remember, we don't always have to describe the actual smell. We can give the character's reaction to it.

(answer page 168)

Compare these sentences. Suggest what Maree might be smelling each time.

1. Maree held her breath and hurried from the room.

____

2. Maree held her nose between her finger and thumb and closed her mouth and eyes.

____

3. Maree raised her nose towards the window and smiled.

____

EXERCISE D

(answer page 168)

Make a list of nouns for types of smells, pleasant and unpleasant (e.g., *stench, aroma*).

_______ _______ _______ _______ _______

EXERCISE E

(answer page 168)

Add to this list of smelling actions (verbs):

detect, sniff, _______ _______ _______ _______

EXERCISE F

(answer page 168)

1. The word *nose* is used when describing the smell of which drink? _______
2. The word *gamy* is used when describing the smell of which food? _______

Writing Tip

Adjectives are useful when describing smells accurately. Rather than write "a bad smell," you could have "a sickening smell" or "an acrid smell."

EXERCISE G

(answer page 168)

1. Keep a list of "smell" adjectives you might like to use or can substitute for words commonly used. Here are some to start you off: *rotten, sweet, fragrant, reeking*.

_______ _______ _______ _______ _______ _______

2. Choose words that these adjectives might describe.

fragrant _______ rancid _______ spicy _______

stale _______ smoky _______ fruity _______

EXERCISE H

(answer page 168)

Give one or two suitable "smell" words to use when writing about these objects/situations. One has been done for you.

Object	Smell Words
old clothes	musty, damp
swamp	______________________________
pine needles	______________________________

"SMELL" WORDS

Smells don't have to be totally pleasant or unpleasant. There are "smell" words (nouns) that may go in between two extremes. Look at the range of words between the extremes of *stench* and *fragrant.*

stench, stink, stale, aroma, bouquet, **fragrance**

←――――――――――――――――――――→

It's these in-between words that are often more useful and descriptive.

EXERCISE I

(answer page 168)

Use your thesaurus to find one or two synonyms (words with similar meanings) for these "smell" words.

aroma ______________ ______________

foul ______________ ______________

putrid ______________ ______________

waft ______________ ______________

bouquet ______________ ______________

whiff ______________ ______________

EXERCISE J

(answer page 168)

Use your dictionary to find the meaning for these "smell" words.

nauseating ______________________________

____

fusty ______________________________

____

noisome ______________________________

____

deodorize ______________________________

____

EXERCISE K

Find four other "smell" words and give the dictionary meaning for them.

1. ____________: ______________________________
2. ____________: ______________________________
3. ____________: ______________________________
4. ____________: ______________________________

EXERCISE L

(answer page 168)

Read this passage and highlight all the "smell"-type words or phrases.

> He became aware of a faint bubbling sound and detected the pungent smell of grease and hot soap from the direction of the kitchen. The kitchen itself stank like a Victorian workhouse laundry. A pail of tea cloths was simmering on the old-fashioned gas stove. In the bustle of departure Dot Moxon must have forgotten to turn off the gas. The gray linen was billowing above the dark, evil smelling scum . . .

From: *The Black Tower* by P.D. James

EXERCISE M

(answer page 168)

What are these items and what are they used for?

mothballs ______________________________

____

____

incense ______________________________

____

____

lavender ______________________________

____

____

EXERCISE N

(answer page 168)

List a few "smell" words that might be used to describe this feast (or a festive meal of your choice).

____

____

____

____

18 Using All the Senses—What Do You Taste?

The sense of taste is one of the least used senses in story writing. It doesn't play a large part in our everyday living, although this doesn't mean we are unconcerned about the taste of food we eat. The sense of taste is a very personal sense.

There are four basic taste sensations: **sweet, sour, bitter,** and **salty**–as well as variations of these (e.g., *bland, tasteless,* and *savory*).

(answer page 168)

Read this passage and note how the author has made use of the sense of taste. Highlight the words that you think refer to tasting.

> Joanna didn't feel hungry. She continued to sit at the breakfast table looking at her burned toast spread with tasteless butter and sickly, sweet raspberry jam. What would she give for something a little bit savory? Maybe a mouth-watering bite of a spicy hamburger with the tang of Spanish onions? Then maybe a rich, medium-rare steak topped with peppery sauce?

Writing Tip

We don't always have to describe the actual taste. We can give the character's reaction to it.

EXERCISE B

(answer page 168)

Compare these sentences, and place a checkmark by the one you think has the greater impact.

1. April put some food into her mouth and chewed it slowly and deliberately.
2. April took a morsel of sauce, held it in her mouth for a few seconds, and then shuddered.

Briefly explain your choice.

____

____

____

____

____

EXERCISE C

(answer page 168)

Make a list of nouns for types of taste–pleasant and unpleasant (e.g., *flavor, tang*).

____

EXERCISE D

(answer page 168)

Add to this list of "taste"-type action words (verbs): *nibble, savor,* __________ __________

__________ __________ __________ __________ __________ __________

EXERCISE E

(answer page 168)

Make a list of "taste" adjectives (e.g., *appetizing, tasty, sickly, sweet*).

____

EXERCISE F

(answer page 168)

Choose words that these adjectives might describe.

delicious __________ tasteless __________ hot (spicy) __________

stale __________ minty __________ sour __________

EXERCISE G

(answer page 169)

1. What drink has a taste that is described as sweet or dry? __________

2. What food has a taste that is described as sweet and sour? __________

EXERCISE H

(answer page 169)

Give one or two suitable "taste" words you can use when writing about the objects/situations in the table on page 74. One has been done for you.

18 USING ALL THE SENSES—WHAT DO YOU TASTE?

Object	Taste Words
chili peppers	spicy, hot
weak juice	________________
freshly baked bread	________________

EXERCISE I

(answer page 169)

Use your thesaurus to find one or two synonyms (words with similar meanings) for these "taste" words.

bland __________ __________ unripe __________ __________

sample __________ __________ tart __________ __________

tasty __________ __________ luscious __________ __________

EXERCISE J

(answer page 169)

Use your dictionary to find the meaning of these "taste" words.

aftertaste ____________________

taste buds ____________________

flat ____________________

sweet tooth ____________________

masticate ____________________

EXERCISE K

Write a paragraph about the taste of a meal you enjoyed.

EXERCISE L

Write a paragraph about the taste of a meal you didn't enjoy.

____

____

____

____

____

____

____

____

____

EXERCISE M

(answer page 169)

Using the correct word is important. What animals would you associate with these eating actions?

nibbling ____________ tearing ____________ gnawing ____________

pecking ____________ lapping ____________ cracking ____________

EXERCISE N

Use the above words or other animal eating action words in a paragraph about either a rural scene or feeding time at the zoo.

Title: ____________________

____

____

____

____

____

____

____

____

____

EXERCISE O

(answer page 169)

1. What is meant by the phrase "turn the stomach"? ____________________

____

2. What are people reacting to when they lick their lips? ____________________

____

EXERCISE P

(answer page 169)

Give a tasting word (noun, verb, or adjective) for these foods and drinks.

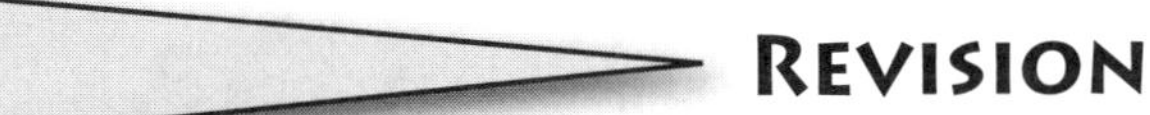

Revision

Direct speech is when the writer uses the actual words spoken. The words spoken are in quotation marks. For example:

Bill replied, "I can let you have one dollar, not more."

Some publishers use single quotation marks (' ') while others prefer double marks (" "). Your teachers will tell you what is required in your school writing.

Indirect speech is often called **reported speech**. The writer uses past tense to report what was said. It is often used in newspaper reports with the word *that* in front of it. For example:

The president said that taxes had to rise.

Exercise A

(answer page 169)

Rewrite these sentences as indirect speech.

1. Bob said, "Today is my birthday, and I am thirteen."

___

2. "Our family is going to Las Vegas for a vacation," stated Jillian.

___

3. "You cannot bring those animals inside," snapped Bill.

___

Writing Tip

Varying the type of speech used in written work can add interest to story writing. It can also get the writer out of situations where finding the exact, correct, or sincere sounding words is difficult.

Exercise B

(answer page 169)

Compare the examples of direct and indirect speech on page 78. Complete example 4 by changing it to indirect speech.

1. "I am very sad to hear about your father's illness and the difficult time he is having," said my friend. OR My friend said that she was saddened by my father's illness.
2. Fran said, "Yes, I can help you with that." OR Fran agreed to help.
3. The builder said, "It is really quite easy to make a dog kennel. First, you get a long piece of timber and cut off one-yard lengths. Then, you nail or bolt them together to make a triangular shape. These will be the frame for the roof . . ." OR The builder explained how to make a dog kennel.
4. The policeman explained, "The suspect was walking along Main Street in a westerly direction when he stopped in front of Sparkler Jeweler. He took an iron bar, which he had hidden under a long coat . . ." OR

____

____

____

EXERCISE C

(answer page 169)

Read these short sentences that you may be able to vary and use in your writing.

Highlight the words that are used as "said"-type words.

1. Janis agreed to go.
2. Frank objected to my request.
3. Paul conceded that I was right.
4. Sue took offense at my suggestion.
5. The doctor concluded that I was well.
6. Father thanked me.
7. Peter dismissed my claim.
8. The teacher greeted the class.

EXERCISE D

In your own words, complete these sentences with indirect speech.

1. Janis agreed ______________________________
2. Frank objected ______________________________

EXERCISE E

(answer page 169)

Rewrite these long sentences as a shorter sentence without direct speech.

Example: Jan looked at her watch and said, "You must stop writing now."

Jan looked at her watch and told us to stop writing.

1. Tony said, "Thank you," as I gave him the bat.

____

2. The producer yelled, "Sam, get off that stage at once."

____

3. "To fix the clock, first take the back off, and then look for the fault," explained Della.

____

EXERCISE F

(answer page 169)

Use your dictionary to find the meanings of these "said" words.

confirm ____

volunteer ____

insist ____

recite ____

dictate ____

EXERCISE G

(answer page 169)

Highlight the words in parentheses that best suit these sentences.

1. "Touch that money, and you'll be sorry," (threatened, granted, proposed) the guard.
2. "Have you a dollar for a sick, old man?" (pleaded, begged, offered) the homeless man.
3. "You can return the papers now," (reported, directed, proclaimed) the examiner.
4. "All you do is watch television and more television," (complained, ordered, roared) his wife.
5. "Can I help you?" (offered, promised, suggested) the shop assistant.

WRITING DIRECT SPEECH

People often speak informally. They don't normally talk in full (formal) sentences or even use grammar correctly all the time. They often leave out the less important words.

Much of what is understood is not actually said.

EXERCISE H

(answer page 169)

Compare these two passages, and place a checkmark by the one that sounds more authentic.

Passage 1 ☐

"Have you been to the store yet?" asked Glen's mother.

"No," replied Glen, "but I'll be going in a minute."

"The store will be closing soon," warned his mother.

"I know that!" growled Glen.

Passage 2 ☐

"Been to the store yet?" asked Glen's mother.

Glen replied, "In a minute."

"Store closes soon," warned his mother.

"I know!" growled Glen.

EXERCISE I

Write a short informal discussion between Guy and Linda, who have just seen the latest box-office hit action movie, *The Last Days of Earth*.

Be sure to start each change of speaker on a new line.

____

____

____

____

____

____

____

____

EXERCISE J

(answer page 169)

Read this short passage and comment on what the writer has done.

> Between popping chips into his mouth Angus described how he scored. "The ball came across from half court, and I cut it off before Jones could trap it. I did a quick dribble around the full back and struck for goal. Got it in with a bounce off the corner post. Great shot! Should have seen his face!"

____

____

____

The characters in your stories may be good or bad people, criminals or angels. Many writers base their characters loosely on people they know. Characters have a physical appearance, habits, emotions, and a cultural heritage that makes each one unique.

Writing Tip

Some writers make a list of the physical features of their characters (e.g., freckles, bald, stubby). Another way to keep track of their features is to cut a picture of the type of character you want from a magazine, newspaper, or comic. Keep it near you when you are writing your story.

EXERCISE A

(answer page 169)

1. Give one character feature of Harry Potter (author: J.K. Rowling): ____________________
2. Give one character feature of Bart Simpson (television cartoon character): ______________

Using real people

Basing a fictional character on a known person has hidden dangers, especially as you get older and your writing becomes more public. It is safer not to use people who are readily recognized, especially if your work might be published and you haven't been kind.

Most of the characters in my longer books are based *loosely* on real people. I decide on a certain type of person (grumpy, giggly, thoughtful, irresponsible) and select a particular "body" for that character. Then I start changing things to make the character fictional and more interesting, but I keep a mental picture of the person. Finally, I decide on a name (see Chapter 21).

Be consistent

The most important thing for your character to be is consistent. Sudden changes in character upset the reader. If your character starts off as cowardly, then don't give them sudden, unexpected moments of bravery. There have to be real reasons for character changes. These become part of your story.

EXERCISE B

Complete the table on page 82. Don't name the real person you have selected as your model, just keep them in mind. "Said" words refers to how they would say something. "Went" words refers to how they might "walk." (See Chapters 25–27 for more on "said," "look," and "went" words.)

Type	Real Person	Gender	Age	Shape	"Said" Words	"Went" Words
quiet	Alan H.	M	50+	chubby	suggest	stroll
bragging	X					
bully	X					
clumsy	X					
fragile	X					

Of course, you can add a lot more points. One of my characters always wore a red scarf, another one joked a lot, and another was a little bit accident-prone.

EXERCISE C

(answer page 169)

1. Select a character type to fit these "went" (walk) action words.

hobble: old man

strut: ____________

dawdle: ____________

prowl: ____________

stumble: ____________

tip-toe: ____________

2. Select a character type to fit these "said" words.

questioned: ____________

pleaded: ____________

murmured: ____________

claimed: ____________

whined: ____________

requested: ____________

3. Select a character type to fit these "look" words.

peruse: ____________

glare: ____________

gape: ____________

squint: ____________

investigate: ____________

glance: ____________

Checklist for Developing Characters

Many writers use a checklist like this (often called a characterization tool).

- → Physical appearance
- → Movements, gestures, and habits (good and bad)
- → Behavior towards others
- → Attitude to others/attitude of other characters to the character
- → Dialogue (way he/she speaks)
- → Physical environment/setting where he/she lives
- → Character's past
- → Minor features (name, preferred clothing, favorite television shows/foods)

EXERCISE D

(answer page 170)

Using this table, fill in details of two characters you might write about.

Checklist Point	Male Character	Female Character
Physical appearance	______________________	______________________
Movements	______________________	______________________
Behavior toward others	______________________	______________________
Dialogue	______________________	______________________
Physical environment	______________________	______________________
Character's past	______________________	______________________
Name	______________________	______________________

EXERCISE E

(answer page 170)

One of the great character creators of English literature was Charles Dickens. Even if you haven't read any of his books, you may have seen movies based on his stories. Scrooge from *A Christmas Carol* is a favorite.

On page 84 list three of Dickens's books (or movies) and a character or two from the story.

Book (Movie)	Character 1	Character 2
______	______	______
______	______	______
______	______	______

EXERCISE F

(answer page 170)

Write some points about each of these characters. Give the character a name.

Name: ______

Likes: ______

______

Dislikes: ______

______ Occupation: ______

Name: ______

Likes: ______

______

Dislikes: ______

______ Occupation: ______

EXERCISE G

(answer page 170)

A character's attitude towards other people is important because it will determine how they act/react. What is the difference between an introvert and an extrovert?

______

______

Giving Characters Names

Some writers are concerned over the names of the characters in their stories. Getting the right sounding name can be important. Christine or Christopher might not be suitable for a child from a place such as India or China.

Try to find names that **suit the character**. In *Dr. awKwarD*, a book about palindromes (words that read the same forward and backwards) I had characters called Hannah and Bob.

Exercise A

(answer page 170)

Highlight the names you think are more suitable for adults in your stories. Remember, names can go in and out of fashion.

Ronald	Beryl	James	Wilma	Ralph	Dorothy	Ian
Kay	Roger	Guy	Dee	Skye	Doreen	Kip

Exercise B

(answer page 170)

With children you can often get away with nicknames (e.g., Blue, Ginger, Skip, Macca).

List some fun nicknames you know.

_______________ _______________ _______________ _______________ _______________

_______________ _______________ _______________ _______________ _______________

Names, Names, Names, Names

Look for unusual names. You can also be adventurous. Skip the Johns and Marys. There are many unusual names around such as Storm, Tiger Lily, Reef, Cyclone, Rainbow, Magic, or Blaze.

I have three books of names. The good thing about name books is that they give the meaning or origin of names. I have a character call Brian. Brian means brave, but my Brian is only brave in his daydreams! I have a character called Calvin, which means bald. He was the hair robber in *The Great Hair Robbery*.

I have another older character called Rex King. He is a lone scientist on a deserted island (in *The Rats of Wolfe Island*). *Rex* is another word for king.

EXERCISE C

Here are some common names and their meanings:

Felicity: happy	George: farmer	Kim: a ruler
Paul: small	Errol: wanderer	Eve: life

What is your name? ______________________________

What does it mean? ______________________________

Writing Tip

It may be wise to check out what your characters' names actually mean. It would be unwise to have two girls in the one family with the names of Liza and Beth, because they are both variations of Elizabeth.

EXERCISE D

(answer page 170)

How many variations of the name Robert can you find?

____

EXERCISE E

(answer page 170)

Make a list of two or three names you might use later for:

1. Older males: ______________________________
2. Older females: ______________________________
3. Teenage girls: ______________________________
4. Teenage boys: ______________________________
5. Mischievous children: ______________________________
6. Weird characters: ______________________________

Writing Tip

It's important to avoid character names that sound or look similar, such as Kirsty and Kristy or Lorna and Laura. Similar sounding names may confuse your reader.

Finding Names

I find a good place for finding names is in the credits of a movie (that part at the end where they list everybody that ever had anything to do with the movie)!

For interesting last names, I often look up the telephone directory. That's how I found the family name (surname) Twentyman that I used in *The Ghost Writer*.

EXERCISE F

Use a telephone directory to find five unusual family names that you could use.

_______________ _______________ _______________ _______________ _______________

Alliteration and Rhyming

Alliteration (two or more words that repeat a similar sound) and rhyming can be useful tools to give a hint as to how you want your reader to interpret the character. It would be hard to take Ian Bean or Cilla Miller (rhyming) seriously. Matthew Myers (alliteration) might be a little more serious.

Of course, you can have real fun with names like Sandy Shaw, Crystal Ball, Rocky Hills, Penny Farthing, Bob Downes, Isobel Silver, Theresa Green, and Justin Case.

EXERCISE G

(answer page 170)

1. Invent three or four characters whose first and last names rhyme.

____

____

____

____

2. Invent four characters whose first and last names are examples of alliteration.

____

____

____

____

3. Invent a name for an awkward kid who is always reading comics. _______________

____

EXERCISE H

(answer page 170)

1. Flowers are often used as first names. Add four more flower names:

Heather ________ ________ ________ ________

2. List four more colors that could be used as first names:

Amber ________ ________ ________ ________

3. List four more places that could be used as first names:

Craig ________ ________ ________ ________

4. List four more occupations that could be used as family names or surnames:

Carpenter ________ ________ ________ ________

EXERCISE I

Think of some names for your characters that would be fun or interesting, and then describe the character.

Character's Name	Description
1. ________	________ ________
2. ________	________ ________
3. ________	________ ________
4. ________	________ ________

Some student writers have no clear idea of just what goes into creating a person. It is sometimes said that their characters are 2-D (two-dimensional) and not 3-D (three-dimensional). The characters have no depth. They are there for the plot and don't have any other reason for existing.

Before you start writing, imagine what makes your character tick. Is he or she shy, confident, thoughtful, caring, moody, and so on? And, of course, they may not act like that throughout the story. A character might be shy with adults but less shy with people his or her own age.

EXERCISE A

Make a list of the types of characters you could include in your stories.

proud, ____________, ____________, ____________, ____________, ____________, ____________

nervous, ____________, ____________, ____________, ____________, ____________, ____________

Being consistent

Once you have decided on your character's character you have to make sure his or her actions and speech reflect the type of character. How would a timid man react to a policeman? How would an impatient girl react in a new class?

Although your characters should behave consistently, they do not have to display their main characteristic all the time. A grumpy person is allowed to smile. A quiet person might be stirred to make a noise by excitement or anger.

EXERCISE B

(answer page 170)

Next to the character types below and on page 90, write down a type of behavior that you might expect from such a character.

Character Type	Action
bold	speaks loudly
lazy	leaves clothes on floor
thoughtless	____________

Character Type	Action
ungrateful	______________
cheeky	______________
disorganized	______________
selfish	______________
calm	______________

EXERCISE C

(answer page 170)

You don't always have to tell the reader what sort of character the person has. You can let the reader work that out from the behavior of the character.

1. How would you describe the character in this short passage? ______________

   Andrew knew what to do. He put his dirty dishes on the sink. He wiped the table where he had been sitting and pushed the chair in, without scratching the floor. After switching off the kitchen light, he went to the bathroom to brush his teeth.

2. There can be shades of character types. Can you think of some character types that could fit between a calm person and an angry person? ______________, ______________

USING SPEECH

One of the most important ways of revealing a person's character is what they say and how they say it (see Chapter 25). Compare these characters showing their annoyance:

"Stop doing that," said Janet.

"Do you mind?" hissed Penny.

The second example provides readers with more information.

EXERCISE D

(answer page 170)

Compare these sentences and place a checkmark by the one you think has the *least* impact.

1. "I'm going home," said Margie.
2. "I'm going home," snapped Margie.
3. "Going home!" growled Margie.

Briefly explain your choice. ____

____

EXERCISE E

(answer page 170)

1. Write your own "said" words in the spaces and note how the meaning changes.

"I can't do that," ______________ Grandpa. "I can't do that," ______________ Grandpa.

"I can't do that," ______________ Grandpa. "I can't do that," ______________ Grandpa.

2. Put suitable "said" words in the spaces for these speakers. Try to imagine the situation in which they might say the words.

"What are you doing here?" ______________ the schoolteacher.

"What are you doing here?" ______________ her best friend.

"What are you doing here?" ______________ my mother as she came into my room.

"What are you doing here?" ______________ the swimming coach.

"What are you doing here?" ______________ the policeman.

3. Select a suitable type of person to say these sentences.

"Did your mommy carry your bag?" sneered the ________________ .

"I have an apple for you," beamed the ________________ .

"Who's next?" called the ________________ .

EXERCISE F

(answer page 170)

How might different people tell someone to leave a room? Look at these examples.

"Get out of here at once!" snarled my big sister.

"Get lost!" ordered Oliver.

"You may be excused," smiled the teacher.

"No children allowed in here," advised the museum attendant.

"Take those smelly pups from here right now," cautioned the grim-faced nurse.

"You are no longer welcome," warned the librarian.

In the examples on the previous page, who was the friendliest person? ____________________

EXERCISE G

(answer page 170)

Different characters also speak in different ways. Some people speak quickly, some mumble, some have bad speech.

1. Here are a few ways people might speak: softly, carefully, with a lisp, with a stutter, with unfinished sentences, repeating themselves, rudely. Add other ways to the list.

____________________, ____________________, ____________________, ____________________

2. Different characters also "move" in different ways. Some people shuffle, some people strut, some people amble. Here are a few ways people might "move": quickly, carefully, with a skip, angrily. Add other ways of moving to the list.

____________________, ____________________, ____________________, ____________________

EXERCISE H

(answer page 171)

Use your dictionary to find the meanings of these character words.

bumptious ____________________

meticulous ____________________

insincere ____________________

staunch ____________________

demanding ____________________

SUMMARY

There are many pointers to the type of person the character in a story might be. They can be very obvious things (such as age, gender, and cultural background), or the pointers can be much more specific (the type of clothes a person wears, their hairstyle, the way they speak, their sport, hobbies, attitude to people and situations).

Who am I?

I am a small, furry, male TV animal. I am very likeable, and I like playing tricks. I am a bit of a show-off. I have lots of energy, and I think I am clever. I often get into trouble, but I can usually talk my way out of it.

Who am I? ____________________ **(Answer is on page 171.)**

Showing, Not Telling 23

Many writers try to tell the reader too much and often too quickly. Readers are intelligent people with imagination and experiences, which a good writer will allow them to use. It also helps to arouse the reader's interest if you don't tell them everything at once.

EXERCISE A

(answer page 171)

Compare these two passages and complete the exercises.

Passage 1

Leon stood perfectly still. The field was dark, but he could see several shadowy shapes to his right. He stared into the darkness. They didn't move. Then he realized what they were. Fence posts!

Passage 2

Leon stood very still in the dark field until he realized the shapes were fence posts.

Which passage best draws the reader into the story? ______________________________

Explain your choice: ______________________________

____

____

____

EXERCISE B

(answer page 171)

Read this short passage.

Several motorcycles were lined up, straining and growling, like runners waiting for a starting gun. The lights changed. There was a gutsy roar and then the smell of burned rubber.

1. What do you think is happening? ______________________________

____

____

2. What does "burned rubber" refer to? ______________________________

____

____

EXERCISE C

(answer page 171)

Read these sentences and briefly answer the questions.

1. The policemen went to the front and knocked boldly. As the door opened, they quickly stepped back.

What is about to happen? ____________________

What are the policemen feeling? ____________________

2. The small Piper aircraft lurched in the storm. The pilot blinked rapidly and wiped his sweaty brow. He found a plastic bottle beside the seat and fumbled with the cap.

What is the pilot feeling? ____________________

What is in the bottle? ____________________

Why did he blink several times? ____________________

3. Andrew came to the jungle's edge. He looked into dim greenness and shuddered.

Why did Anthony shudder? ____________________

EXERCISE D

(answer page 171)

Add a sentence to each of the examples to **show** the feeling in parentheses. For example:

Mary was just finishing the question when she saw Brett looking over her shoulder. (annoyance)

She slammed her book shut.

1. Ken heard the waves rolling up the narrow beach. (cold)

____

2. George handed the opened letter to the lawyer. (satisfaction)

____

3. I entered the dressing room without looking at the door sign. (embarrassment)

____

4. Father returned from the hospital late at night. (worry)

____

5. Roderick put the last bag of cement on the truck. (fatigue)

____

6. The coach watched his team leave the court. (disappointment)

____

7. Peter opened the exam booklet and read the first question. (dread)

____

8. At the park Jenny watched dog trainers teach the dogs tricks. (amusement)

____

EXERCISE E

(answer page 171)

This time, "show" different responses to the same lead-in sentence.

1. Lindy, with the key in her hand, climbed the steps to her front door. (relief)

____

2. Lindy, with the key in her hand, climbed the steps to her front door. (anger)

____

3. Lindy, with the key in her hand, climbed the steps to her front door. (weariness)

____

4. Lindy, with the key in her hand, climbed the steps to her front door. (puzzlement)

____

5. Lindy, with the key in her hand, climbed the steps to her front door. (tiredness)

____

EXERCISE F

(answer page 171)

Read these sentences and write in the space what you think the person is feeling.

1. Gwen moved her face closer to the monitor and rubbed her eyes. ______________

____

2. Ari stopped at the gate, checked his watch, put his hand on the gatepost, and then looked at his watch again. ____________________

3. There were eight mice in their boxes, ready for the start of a race. Mike looked at Buster Malloy's mouse and frowned. ____________________

4. Lee watched Sue start chewing the gum she had given her. Suddenly, Lee hunched her shoulders and covered her mouth with her hand. ____________________

5. As she slowly opened the lid, Kate peered into the old chest. For a moment, she just stared and then she let the lid drop with a sudden thud. ____________________

EXERCISE G

(answer page 171)

Rewrite these sentences so that you show and **do not tell**. For example:

The blue cattle dog snarled at the cat with cruel **menace**.

The blue cattle dog snarled at the cat and bared its moist fangs.

1. The fly zoomed around Ms. Green's lunchbox, and she was **annoyed**.

____

____

2. While sitting in the waiting room, Pete became very **bored** indeed.

____

____

3. As he walked home, Jason got quite **hot**.

____

____

4. Pauline was **pleased**. She saw her name on the list of competition winners.

____

____

5. René was **puzzled** as she watched the kitten at the top of the pole.

____

____

Selecting a Point of View

Before you start writing, you should consider who is telling the story. If your story is in **first person**, that is, the narrator is telling the story, then the story is from his or her viewpoint. In first person narrative, the writer uses such words as *I, me, her,* and *we* (pronouns) throughout the story.

Read this short passage written in first person. The personal pronouns are in **bold**.

> It all started innocently enough. **I** was on summer vacation and Mom had been planning a few "educational" activities for **me**. On this particular day **she** had decided **we** should visit the Powerhouse Museum to check out the new electronics exhibition. **We** caught a train into Town Hall Station then boarded one of the monorail trains at Park Plaza.
>
> From: *Monopillar*

EXERCISE A

(answer page 171)

Highlight the pronouns in this sentence:

> When I see Marnie, I will tell her that you are staying with an auntie of mine.

First person stories

If your story is in first person, then all the action is limited to what the narrator can see, hear, and experience. It is impossible to see into the minds of other characters but first person narrative can create closer contact with the reader. Diary-type stories are in first person. They are personal records of events and feelings (e.g., *So Much to Tell You* by John Marsden, *Penny Pollard's Diary* by Robyn Klein).

RESEARCH

(answer page 171)

1. Go to your library and list four books written in first person (e.g., *Treasure Island* by Robert Louis Stevenson, *The Gizmo* by Paul Jennings, *Tales of a Fourth Grade Nothing* by Judy Blume).

   ______________________ ______________________

   ______________________ ______________________

2. Do you know of a writer who regularly writes in first person? ______________________

3. Find a copy of *Lake at the End of the World* by Caroline Macdonald. The story is told in first person from two different viewpoints. What has this enabled the author to do?

   ____

   ____

   ____

Other Approaches

Many stories are told in **third person** from the viewpoint of one or more of the characters. These stories are told as if the reader is watching the events that are happening and knows what is going on in the character's mind. *Charlotte's Web*, by E.B. White, is told from Charlotte's viewpoint and at times from Fern's viewpoint, in alternating chapters.

In your stories you may take the **"overall" viewpoint**. The main character often sees or knows what is going on in other people's minds. Changes in setting are easily brought into the story.

Writing Tip

The danger with the "overall" approach is that the writer can give too much away, not allowing the readers to draw on their own experiences and imagination.

EXERCISE B

There is about to be an accident on the intersection of Main Street and High Street. There are at least ten people somehow involved in the event. In a few sentences write what is happening from three different points of view. Select a character from each category (1, 2, 3) below. Highlight your choice in each case.

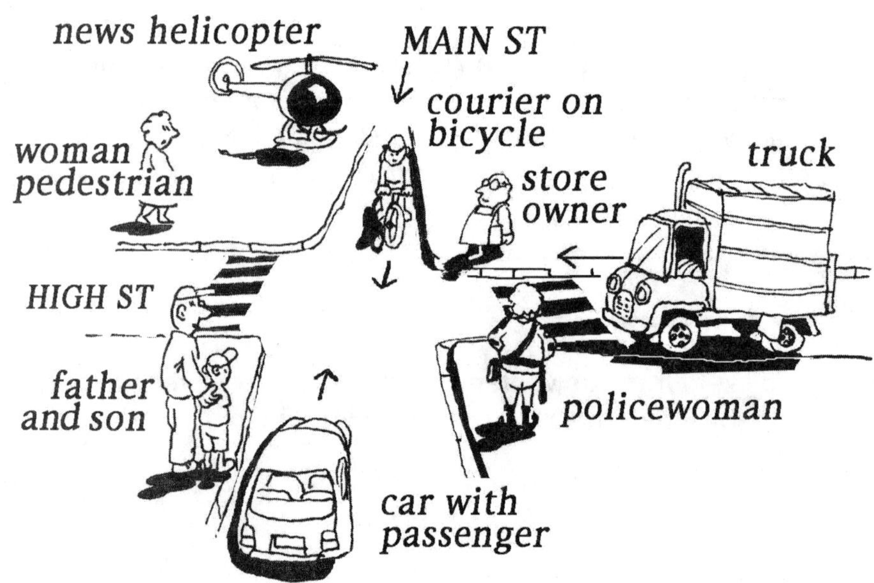

1. **Third person**: driver of truck, driver of car, father, child, passenger

____

____

____

____

2. **First person**: policewoman, female pedestrian , store owner, child, courier

3. **"Overall viewpoint"**: the news reporter in the helicopter, pilot

EXERCISE C

(answer page 171)

Read these passages and determine the viewpoint. Write your selection in the space below.

I let out a noise that would have told the whole world I was about to be sick. Without thinking, I stood and stumbled forwards, trying to wipe the smelly gunk off my face. Then I fell into the bulging garbage bags.

They rattled and burst open as I tried to get up.

From: *Monopillar*

1. ______________________

But Brian was not afraid. He was strong and powerful. He took a small chair and walked towards the largest lion with the huge head and magnificent flowing mane. He pointed the legs at the lion. The lion jumped onto a large yellow barrel.

He made the next two lions jump through hoops. The people clapped.

From: "Dream on, Brian"

2. ______________________

Across the stalk land, into the pine wood, into the climbing, brightening glow of the dawn, the boy followed the dog, whose anxious pace slowed from age as they went. "By a dog's age, Sounder is past dying time," the boy said half aloud. Fear had always prompted him to talk to himself.

From: *Sounder* by W.H. Armstrong

3. ______________________

FINDING OTHER WORDS FOR "SAY" 25

When using speech in your story writing, it is very easy and convenient to use the word *said*. It can also become monotonous.

Try to find "say"-type words that contain shades of meaning to indicate the way a speaker is talking. For example, take these words: *yelled, shouted, called, screamed, bellowed*. They all mean talking loudly but each one carries its own additional information.

Writing Tip

A good thesaurus is a must! Many computer programs have a built-in thesaurus, but many are fairly basic (as yet). You also still need a dictionary.

(answer page 172)

Read these speech sentences. Notice how much more impact the bold words have than *said* would have. They give the reader some idea of the speaker's feelings and attitude. They also give the reader some insight into the character of the speaker.

"That was the last game I will ever play in this team," **growled** the suspended player.

"That was the last game I will ever play in this team," **sighed** the retiring player.

"That was the last game I will ever play in this team," **admitted** the injured goalie.

"That was the last game I will ever play in this team," **teased** the captain.

What is each person feeling?

1. suspended player: ____________________
2. retiring player: ____________________
3. injured goalie: ____________________
4. captain: ____________________

ORDER OF WORDS

The quoted words of the speaker need not start the sentence. For variety, the quoted words can come after we are told who is speaking. Compare these two sentences:

"How far to the next crossroads?" asked the driver.

The driver asked, "How far to the next crossroads?"

EXERCISE B

(answer page 172)

Find a variety of suitable "said" words to complete these sentences.

1. "Turn that oven off, now!" ______________________ the chef.

2. "Oh, I hope it's not another storm coming," ______________________ the upset camper.

3. The children ______________________ , "We've got your bag. We've got your bag."

4. "But this packet has been opened," ______________________ the customer.

5. "Give it to me!" ______________________ the goalie. "I'll clear it to left field."

Writing Tip

With each change of speaker, you must start a new paragraph. Some publishers indent each new paragraph, others don't.

EXERCISE C

Here is a list of words that are used as alternatives to *said*. Here it is as an alphabetical selection. Many classrooms have a list on the wall. Add your own "said" words in the spaces.

a	added	______________________	j	joked	______________________
b	barked	______________________	k	kidded	______________________
c	claimed	______________________	l	lectured	______________________
d	denied	______________________	m	mentioned	______________________
e	explained	______________________	n	niggled	______________________
f	forgave	______________________	o	offered	______________________
g	greeted	______________________	p	prayed	______________________
h	hinted	______________________	q	quipped	______________________
i	insisted	______________________	r	recited	______________________

s snorted ____________

t teased ____________

u uttered ____________

v volunteered ____________

w whined ____________

x ? ____________

y yapped ____________

z zapped ____________

EXERCISE D

(answer page 172)

Use your dictionary to find the meaning of these "said" words.

lecture ____________

harangue ____________

blurt ____________

rave ____________

coax ____________

interrogate ____________

EXERCISE E

(answer page 172)

Use your thesaurus to find two words of similar meaning to these "said" words.

concur ____________ ____________

repeat ____________ ____________

notify ____________ ____________

whoop ____________ ____________

divulge ____________ ____________

EXERCISE F

(answer page 172)

Fill the spaces in this short passage with a variety of different "said" words. Make your "said" word suit the character or the situation.

"What have you found?" _______________ David as Leo stood up.

Leo held a small object up to the light and _______________ , "It looks like a small gold nugget."

"Can't be," _______________ David. "This is limestone country."

"Someone might have dropped it," _______________ Leo, looking directly at David.

"Yeah, your bank manager!" _______________ David with a smirk.

Leo _______________ , "Don't try to be smart. It doesn't suit you."

Writing Tip

Sometimes, when only two people are speaking the "said" words may be omitted, speeding up the exchange and making the conversation more urgent, exciting, or tense.

EXERCISE G

(answer page 172)

Read this extract from *Talking in Whispers* by James Watson. In it Andres is being questioned by a military interrogator (Snake). Note how the speakers' names have not been included in this exchange. This adds pace and tension to the interchange. Now read on.

> The pain was too much. "Yes, yes . . . there was a doctor." Andres suffered a further blow. Talking, that keeps their fists away.
>
> "Man or . . . woman?"
>
> "Didn't see."
>
> "Talk!"
>
> "Man!"
>
> "You lie!"
>
> "Man!"

Suggest a "said"-type word to show how "Talk!" might have been said.

____

EXERCISE H

Using the extract in Exercise G as a model, continue this exchange between a bus driver and a student. Keep the exchanges short.

"What's your problem?" the driver asked, looking directly at Yvonne.

"Lost my pass," muttered Yvonne.

EXERCISE I

(answer page 172)

Convert this passage to direct speech. Refer to the list of "say" words on pages 102–103.

Toni proposed that they buy a Harry Potter book for Robert's birthday party.

Jenny didn't think that was a good idea.

Toni asked why she disagreed.

Jenny said that everyone had read all the Harry Potter books.

Toni shook her head. She told Jenny that the latest Harry Potter book had just been released. It had been in the stores for just two days.

EXERCISE J

Write a short interchange between two students planning a way to skip physical education class in the afternoon. Use direct and indirect speech.

FINDING OTHER WORDS FOR "LOOK" 26

Just as overuse of *say* or *said* can become monotonous and is uninformative, to a lesser extent the same can be said for a number of other words, including "look"-type words.

EXERCISE A

(answer page 172)

Read these "look"-type sentences and consider how the character in each is acting. In the space provided, comment briefly on each character's feelings at the time. The first has been done for you.

1. My father **leafed through** a business magazine. thoughtful

2. The teacher **gazed** through the classroom window towards the beach. ________________

3. Anne **inspected** the fillings of the sandwiches in her lunchbox. ________________

4. The captain **glared** at the referee for allowing the penalty. ________________

5. The manuscript was **scrutinized** by the firm's legal adviser. ________________

6. The tired hikers **surveyed** the valley below looking for signs of life. ________________

OTHER WORDS

Notice how much more impact the bold words in the sentences above have than *looked* would have. They give the reader some idea of the character's feelings and attitude.

Words can show different ways a character might "look at" or "see" under different circumstances (e.g., *peeked, stared, examined, inspected*). These are all examples of "looking," but each one carries its own additional information.

EXERCISE B

Make your own alphabetical list of words that are alternatives to *looked*. Some suggestions have been included.

a		______	n		______
b	blinked	______	o	ogled	______
c		______	p		______
d		______	q		______
e	eyed	______	r		______
f		______	s	studied	______
g	gazed	______	t		______
h		______	u		______
i		______	v	viewed	______
j		______	w		______
k		______	x		______
l	leered	______	y		______
m		______	z		______

EXERCISE C

(answer page 172)

Find a variety of suitable "looked/saw" words to complete these sentences.

1. The workers ______________ across the flooded street towards the bus shelter.

2. Dr. Smithers ______________ a small blemish on the patient's eyelid.

3. Sally ____________________ the small print on the carton of smelly milk.

4. Kerry had a sly ____________________ her mother's old baby photos.

5. Francis ____________________ the antics of the monkeys in the treetops.

EXERCISE D

(answer page 172)

Use your dictionary to find the meaning of these "look" words.

browse ______________________________

skim ______________________________

scowl ______________________________

gape ______________________________

grimace ______________________________

gloat ______________________________

behold ______________________________

EXERCISE E

(answer page 172)

Look at these sentences and note how the meaning changes when different "look/see" words are used.

1. Ashley **glanced at** the old timetable at the end of the station.
2. Ashley **studied** the old timetable at the end of the station.
3. Ashley **inspected** the old timetable at the end of the station.

In which sentence does Ashley give little attention to the timetable? ________

In which sentence is Ashley more interested in the timetable information? ________

EXERCISE F

(answer page 172)

Using "look"-type words fill in the blanks in these sentences to get a specific meaning. You may also have to use a preposition, such as *at*.

1. Molly ____________________ the shape as it came through the forest in her direction.
2. Molly ____________________ the shape as it came through the forest in her direction.
3. Molly ____________________ the shape as it came through the forest in her direction.
4. Molly ____________________ the shape as it came through the forest in her direction.
5. Molly ____________________ the shape as it came through the forest in her direction.

EXERCISE G

(answer page 172)

Use your thesaurus to find two words of similar meaning to these "look" words.

frown ____________________ ____________________

review ____________________ ____________________

investigate ____________________ ____________________

look up ____________________ ____________________

glimpse ____________________ ____________________

EXERCISE H

(answer page 172)

We often hear these phrases. Explain what they mean.

looking daggers ____

eyeball to eyeball ____

look-see ____

bird's-eye view ____

EXERCISE I

Using some of your "look"-type words, write a short paragraph about what has upset this character. You can call him Neville.

____

____

____

____

____

____

____

____

____

____

____

EXERCISE J

(answer page 173)

Read this short extract from *Sit Down, Mom, There's Something I've Got to Tell You* by Moya Simons and answer the questions below.

> Suddenly, I spy Giles. He is talking to Susie and has an arm on her shoulder. She's smiling and he's looking right into her eyes. I feel queasy inside.

1. What does the word *spy* suggest about the narrator? ______________________________

____

____

____

2. Why is Giles looking into Susie's eyes? ______________________________

____

____

____

27 Finding Other Words for "Go"

Just as the overuse of *said* can become monotonous and be uninformative, to a lesser extent the same can be said for "go/went"-type words.

Words can show the different ways a character might go from one place to another (e.g., *walked, ambled, strolled, hiked*). These are all examples of words for going somewhere but each one carries its own additional information.

There are also different words for travelling across water and through the air.

EXERCISE A

(answer page 173)

Read these "go/went"-type sentences and notice how much more impact the **bold** words have than *walked/went* would have. They give the reader some idea of the character's feelings and attitude.

In the space provided, comment briefly on each character's feelings at the time. The first has been done for you.

1. The man was so overweight that he **waddled** to the shops. ___awkward___

2. My uncle **shuffled** down the hallway to the bathroom. ____________________

3. The guard **marched** the prisoner back to his cell. ____________________

4. We waited while Lenny **roamed** up and down the supermarket aisles. ____________________

5. The lone explorer **staggered** into the campsite covered in bites and mud. ____________________

6. Farmer Jones **plodded** across the boggy fields. ____________________

7. Amanda **skipped** brightly towards the returning car. ____________________

Which person from the above sentences do you think is the oldest?

____

EXERCISE B

Make your own alphabetical list of words that are alternatives to *went*. Some have been included for you.

a ambled ______
b beetled ______
c careened ______
d ______
e ______
f ______
g ______
h hiked ______
i ______
j ______
k ______
l limped ______
m ______
n ______
o ______
p ______
q ______
r ______
s strolled ______
t trudged ______
u ______
v ______
w walked ______
x ______
y ______
z zoomed ______

EXERCISE C

(answer page 173)

Find a variety of suitable "went"-type words to complete these sentences.

1. Our cat, Bella, ______ across the room to her food bowl.

2. The scouts ______ across the shallow lake to the campsite.

3. The hockey team ____________________ from the dressing rooms onto the field.

4. Simon rented a canoe and ____________________ across the small lake.

5. The weary climbers ____________________ the last few yards to the summit.

EXERCISE D

(answer page 173)

Use your dictionary to find the meaning of these "went" words.

promenade ____

twirl ____

traipse ____

thread ____

frolic ____

trundle ____

romp ____

EXERCISE E

(answer page 173)

Look at these similar sentences and see how the meaning is changed by using different "went"-type words.

1. Peter **crept** through the tall grass on his way to the deserted house.
2. Peter **barged** through the tall grass on his way to the deserted house.
3. Peter **struggled** through the tall grass on his way to the deserted house.
4. Peter **romped** through the tall grass on his way to the deserted house.

Which sentence suggests that Peter had difficulty getting through the grass? ______________

Which sentence suggests that Peter is having fun? ______________

Which sentence suggests that Peter may be doing something scary? ______________

EXERCISE F

(answer page 173)

Using a variety of words fill in the blanks in these sentences to get different meanings.

1. The last contestant ______________ across the field to the waiting judges.
2. The last contestant ______________ across the field to the waiting judges.
3. The last contestant ______________ across the field to the waiting judges.
4. The last contestant ______________ across the field to the waiting judges.
5. The last contestant ______________ across the field to the waiting judges.

EXERCISE G

(answer page 173)

Find suitable "went"-type words to complete these sentences.

1. The eagle ______________ on the mouse as it crept from under the log.
2. The lions ______________ the deer grazing in the long grass.
3. The dancer ______________ across the stage.
4. The snake ______________ along the tree trunk towards the nest.
5. The skier ______________ down the slope to the finish line.

EXERCISE H

(answer page 173)

Use your thesaurus to find two words of similar meaning to these "went" words.

totter ______________ ______________

trek ______________ ______________

range ______________ ______________

lurch ______________ ______________

escort ______________ ______________

EXERCISE I

(answer page 173)

We often hear these terms or phrases. What do they mean?

1. take a stroll ______________________________

2. a rolling stone ______________________________

3. sail the seven seas ______________________________

EXERCISE J

Using some of your "went"-type words write a short paragraph about what this character is doing. You can call her Nancy. She is on her way to the bus stop.

EXERCISE K

(answer page 173)

Read this extract from *Freddie the Frightened* by Pamela Shrapnel and answer the questions below.

Penelope bounded along the railway platform yelling at them in a very large voice.

Fred, who tended to creep carefully to avoid the cracks, was quite overwhelmed.

1. What does the word *bounded* suggest about Penelope? ______________________

2. How would you describe Fred? ______________________

Most stories start with some sort of **problem**—bullying, a murder, finding treasure, getting a boyfriend/girlfriend, a family dispute. This problem has to be solved.

Along the way to solving the problem a number of events take place. These are sometimes called obstacles, **complications**, or crises. I often have three of these in my stories.

Finally, the problem is solved, at the **climax**. The solving of the problem is often called the **resolution**.

Writing Tip

The climax should be the most exciting part of your story. The problem is solved in some way (not necessarily happily)—the murderer is captured, the girl falls in love with the boy, the space travelers return safely home.

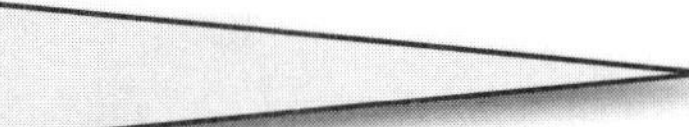

Story Structure

Here is a simple diagram for story writing. All stories do not have to follow this structure.

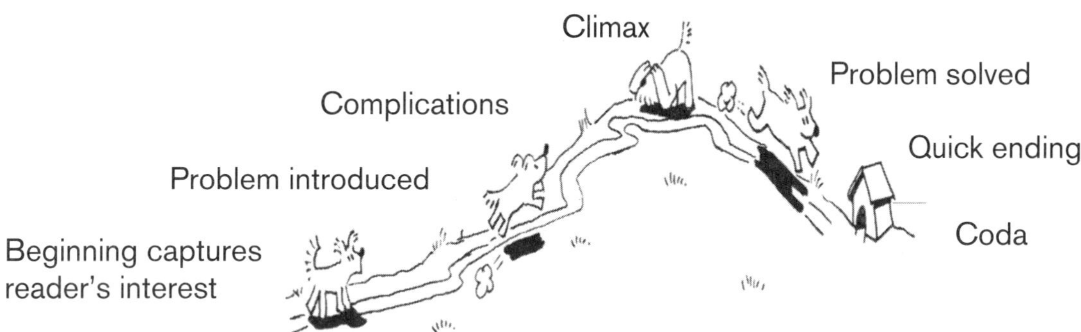

This is the structure of my story *My Sad Skeleton.*

Beginning: Jed opens a box that contains a skeleton (his father is an archaeologist).

Problem: The skeleton is sad and lonely. Jed decides to help the skeleton.

Complications:

1. Jed and the skeleton go for a walk in the park, hoping for inspiration to make the skeleton happy. They are chased out by hungry dogs. Difficulty readily resolved.
2. Jed and the skeleton go to the museum looking for ways to make the skeleton happy. They are chased by museum guards who think Jed is robbing them of an exhibit. This is a larger problem than the first complication.
3. Jed and the skeleton go to a fun fair in an effort to make the skeleton happy.

Climax: Jed and the skeleton are confronted by a very angry sideshow operator. Things seem to have become much worse.

Resolution: The sideshow operator gives the skeleton a job scaring people who ride on his ghost train.

Coda: Jed is joined by his father to wave to the skeleton every time the fun fair is in town.

Writing Tip

The complications on the way to the climax should become more difficult to solve.

EXERCISE A

(answer page 173)

Take the fairytale *The Three Little Pigs* (or a story of your choice), and jot down points as in the example of *My Sad Skeleton.*

Beginning: ______________________________

Problem: ______________________________

Complications: ______________________________

____

Climax: ______________________________

Resolution: ______________________________

Coda: ______________________________

WRITING AN OUTLINE

An **outline** is a short description of the plot of the story that you intend to write.

For school assignments it may be in your head. For longer works and for special situations (exams, projects, competitions), it would be wise to write it down. You can change it later if you come up with more interesting ideas.

The outline for *The Hare and the Tortoise* might go like this:

> A hare brags he is the fastest runner in the forest. He challenges the forest animals to a race. The challenge is accepted by a tortoise. The hare treats the tortoise as a joke. The hare is so confident of winning, he has a rest along the way and goes to sleep. The tortoise wins.

A **synopsis** is a more detailed development of the story. In longer stories it may include what happens in each chapter. It is usually not necessary for school tasks.

EXERCISE B

(answer page 173)

Write a brief outline for the fable *The Lion and the Mouse* (or a story of your choice).

____

____

____

EXERCISE C

(answer page 173)

Can you name the fables based on the outlines below?

A mother duck hatches a number of eggs. From the last egg to hatch emerges a very ugly duckling. It is so ugly, it is picked on by all the other ducklings. The ugly duckling has a very unhappy life. It finally meets some swans who cannot understand its sorrow. They tell it to look at its reflection in the lake. The duckling is no longer an ugly duckling but a graceful swan.

1. ______________________________

A hungry fox sees some grapes hanging high on a vine. They are just what he needs. He tries to jump for the grapes. No matter how hard he tries and how high he jumps, he cannot grab the grapes. Finally, he gives up, declaring that the grapes are sour.

2. ______________________________

EXERCISE D

Write a brief outline for the fairytale *Hansel and Gretel* (or a story of your choice).

Moving the Story Forward

A story must **move forward**. It should move forward with more than just incident after incident. Each complication should be a little more difficult to overcome than the previous one.

We have all seen movies where the main character goes from one disaster to another. These often do little to progress the story. Just how many wild animals can a hunter fight before the end of the film? We get that "oh-not-that-again" feeling.

In a good story, each crisis/complication moves the story forward. For example, in *The Three Little Pigs,* the wolf doesn't just try to get the pigs by blowing each house down one by one. Each new house situation is more complicated than the last. In the first house, only one pig is threatened. In the second house, two pigs are threatened, and so on. Finally, it appears that the desperate wolf has a plan that will succeed.

Flashback

After you have understood that stories start at the beginning and move forward in time, you come across a technique called **flashback**.

Flashback is a technique of starting at some point in the story and then returning to an earlier point in the narrative. It is used effectively in movies when a scene near the beginning fades to an earlier point of time.

In R.L. Stevenson's *Treasure Island,* an older Jim Hawkins has been asked to relate the Treasure Island story. The book then returns to the days when he was a young boy about to get mixed up with pirates and a hunt for treasure. Similarly, in *Del-Del* by Victor Kelleher the story starts four years after "everything started."

The Rats of Wolfe Island begins with Eddie's third and final trip to the island. He is reading the email that prompted his present visit.

> The email was puzzling. No, it was confusing.
>
> I took it from the pocket of my denim jacket and reread the terrible typing. It was more than just the typing, it looked as if it had been written by someone not fully coherent, or as if it had been badly copied.

The story then "flashes back" to his first trip to the island and traces the events of earlier visits. In the actual sequence of events, the first chapter is really the second to the last chapter.

If I were to retell the Goldilocks story using flashback, I might start like this:

> Goldilocks landed heavily on the hard ground. It had been a long jump, and now as she looked up at the window with the three angry bears watching her, she realized just how foolish her early morning walk had been.
>
> Goldilocks had left her parents' home for an early morning walk when she came across . . .

Writing Tip

The advantage of flashback is that the writer can grab the reader's interest, and make them want to know what has happened, by starting in an exciting or intriguing part of the story.

EXERCISE E

Find a book or story that involves flashback. ____________________________________

EXERCISE F

Select a story you know and write a flashback beginning.

Title: ______________________________

29 STRUCTURING A STORY 2

Read the story *Harley* by Alan and Elaine Horsfield and note the features of the narrative.

A narrative is more than a recount. It creates an experience to be shared with the reader, through the characters in the text.

Setting and time are revealed early in narratives.

As a narrative it contains facts, as well as descriptions and atmosphere. Not all information is revealed immediately to the reader.

Narrative contains information about characters' thoughts and past events.

Early in Chapter 1 the author introduces the problem to be solved and creates a mood of uncertainty about the future.

The first crisis: the pet dog feels it has been unfairly tricked by Harley.

Flashback point.

HARLEY

Chapter 1

Harley lay on the dying grass of the lawn playing dreamily with Podgy, the family's little dog. He was rolling a ball back and forth between his hands, and Podgy was trying to snatch it.

It had been a hot, long summer, and Harley had had his share of troubles. He wasn't too sure about the coming days.

Little did he know his mother was watching him from inside the front window of their house. She wasn't too sure about the next days either, after their experiences since the start of school vacation. Not that Harley went to school–yet. Tomorrow would be his first day.

Harley's mom gave a long sigh, just thinking about Harley in class. It wasn't so much that he was a naughty boy. He was, as his father said, accident prone.

As she watched, Harley stood with the ball. Podgy jumped excitedly around his feet. It was game time. Harley's really good with animals, his mother realized as Harley tossed the ball at the brick wall of the house.

Podgy took off after the ball. He jumped into the air to grab it as it unexpectedly bounced off the wall. Podgy missed, made a quick U-turn, and was after the ball as it came to rest in the rose garden.

Podgy had forgotten that roses have thorns!

As he scampered through the foliage, he let out a surprised yelp. Then, for a moment he was very still before backing out of the maze of small branches.

Back on the lawn Podgy started licking his wounds. He looked at Harley with big sad eyes. Harley hurried over to pat Podgy. Podgy was not interested. He limped off to rest on the welcome mat by the front door.

Podgy looked as if he had been unfairly tricked.

Harley looked bewildered.

Harley's mom didn't know what to think.

Then she remembered the start of the summer vacation–and the first signs of trouble.

Chapter 2

It started when Harley's dad got him a slippery-dip. His dad spent hours bolting it together. Finally, it was finished, silvery-blue and very new looking. Harley wanted to try it out immediately, but his father said they had to put sand at the bottom of the slide. He didn't want Harley getting hurt.

Second crisis: the pet dog is nearly squashed by Harley's actions. Short sentences are used for dramatic effect.

Word picture of the event so that the reader can identify with the experience.

Each paragraph adds a new development to the sequence of the story. The story progresses with each new paragraph.

On the whole, events unfold in the order in which they happen —chronologically.

They bought some bags of sand and soon the slippery-dip was ready for hours of fun. It would take his mind off school.

Trouble was, when Podgy saw the soft, clean sand on the grass he just knew it would be the perfect place to sleep.

Little did Harley know, as he balanced at the top of the slide, that Podgy was just out of sight at the flat end of the slide.

"Whoopeee!" yelled Harley as he started sliding. He got faster and faster. It was like flying.

"Whoopeee!" he yelled again. That yell probably saved Podgy's life.

Podgy woke with a start as a large shadow loomed over the sand. Letting out a yelp he made a dash for safety.

Too late! Podgy was caught in a gigantic spray of sand as Harley hit the ground and tumbled over and over, laughing as he went.

He finally ended up with a startled Podgy cradled in his arms.

This was too much for Podgy. After glaring at Harley, he strutted off to the safety of the back steps.

Harley stood up, shook off the loose sand and watched Podgy disappear.

Then Harley did all sorts of things. He went down backwards. He went down sideways. He went down with his hands in the air.

Then he had a brilliant idea. It was hot and he needed to cool off. He decided to turn his slippery-dip into a waterslide.

In no time he had the hose up the ladder and water gushing down the slide.

Then he had another idea. A tummy slide, head first!

But the water had made the slide very slick. No sooner had Harley got into sliding position, and he was away. Whoosh!

The sand at the bottom was very wet. The dirt under the sand was sloppy.

The shower that Harley had to have was warm and full blast. His father waited by the shower, arms folded, until Harley had scrubbed every speck of dirt from his sore body.

Chapter breaks are used to isolate major crises in the plot.

Third crisis. Events between Podgy and Harley become increasingly more dramatic and unstable.

Chapter 3

Later Harley was given a bike as a surprise. Harley knew he could ride even though he had never been on a two-wheel bike.

"Take off the training wheels, Dad," he said. "I don't need them."

His dad looked uncertain but agreed. Then he helped Harley onto the seat.

Harley's feet found the pedals. He knew what to do. He had seen cycle racing on TV!

He suddenly pressed firmly with his front foot.

He was away—straight down the front path. Trouble was, he wasn't too good at steering. And the front gate was looming up fast. He yanked at the handlebars—but much too hard.

He missed the gate. He just missed Podgy who raced to hide in the carport as Harley ended up in a tangle of bicycle on the pansy garden that was in full bloom.

Then there was the time Harley decided the goldfish needed feeding. Harley's mom didn't even want to remember that!

Narrative reverts to the current problem.

The reader is kept in suspense as the parents find out about Harley's first day at school.

Use of questions lets the reader identify with the parents' worries.

The climax comes when Harley is seen leaving the classroom with the teacher.

Sentence starts with conjunction *and* to create a sense of normalcy.

The notion of "a big problem" introduced in Chapter 1 is revisited in the final paragraphs.

Actions and relationships are linked through the use of pronouns.

Final paragraph is a "feel good" ending but is only marginally important to Harley's survival on his first day at school.

But she remembered she had to get Harley's school bag ready.

Harley was off to school.

Chapter 4

At the end of Harley's first school day, his parents waited anxiously in the school grounds.

Harley's new class came out, smiling and laughing.

Where was Harley?

Where was his teacher?

"Oh my," whispered Harley's mom, "I don't like this."

His dad remained silent for a moment before saying, "Look, there's his teacher!"

"She's got Harley by her side!" said his wife grimly. "What's he done?" Harley's mom couldn't stand the stress any longer. She rushed over to the teacher, Ms. Lambert. "Is everything alright?" she begged.

Ms. Lambert looked at her for a moment. "Are you Harley's mother?"

This is it, thought Harley's mom. "Yes," she nodded.

"What a pleasure to meet you," Ms. Lambert said, putting out her hand. "Your son was wonderful in class. Worked all day. Never made a noise. So well behaved. You must be so proud of him."

Harley's mom could hardly keep her mouth from dropping open.

Harley's dad took his bag as they walked to the car in happy silence.

And there was Podgy at the back window, all excited to see Harley again.

"And I thought school was going to be a big problem," said Harley happily.

"I must admit, so did we," said his dad.

Harley didn't see the secret smile that passed between his parents. He was too busy ruffling Podgy's ears.

The organization of much fiction writing follows this sequence:

1. Title
2. Setting (orientation)
3. Problem identified
4. Complications (additional problems)
5. Resolution/climax
6. Rounding off of story (coda)

Writing Tip

Many fiction writers may vary this organization to make their writing original and interesting. For example, a good detective story may start off with the problem (murder or robbery) and reveal the setting later.

EXERCISE A

(answer page 173)

Complete the table below to show the organization of the story you have just read.

1. Title	
2a. Setting (place)	
2b. Setting (time)	
3. Problem	
4. Complication	
5. Climax	
6. Coda	

EXERCISE B

(answer page 173)

Fiction can have a number of purposes. In your opinion, what is the main purpose of the story about Harley? Underline your choice.

- → to educate
- → to entertain
- → to provide a course of action
- → to arouse the reader's emotion
- → to persuade children to behave

EXERCISE C

(answer page 173)

Grammar plays an important part in the telling of a story. Find adjectives used in the story to describe these nouns.

________ summer	________ grass	________ wall
________ smile	________ sand	________ class
________ problem	________ position	________ yelp

EXERCISE D

(answer page 173)

Find adverbs used in the story to enhance these verbs.

playing ________	jumped ________	bounced ________
tricked ________	pressed ________	waited ________

EXERCISE E

(answer page 174)

Give proper nouns from the story for these common nouns.

the boy ________; the dog ________; the teacher ________

EXERCISE F

(answer page 174)

Narratives let the reader see into the mind of characters.

1. What was Harley's mother's belief about Harley and animals?

____

____

2. How did the parents feel as school came out on Harley's first day?

____

____

3. What did Harley's mother try to forget?

____

____

EXERCISE G

(answer page 174)

Complete the following exercises.

1. Circle the word that best describes Harley's feeling about going to school:

   excited   frightened   despondent   puzzled

2. Circle the word that best describes the mother's feeling about Harley and school:

   concerned   impressed   relaxed   despondent

3. What is meant by the term "accident prone"?

   ____

4. When did Harley's run of mishaps begin?

   ____

5. Find a question sentence (not the one underlined) that lets the reader identify with the feelings of one of the characters.

   ____

6. Give an example of a short sentence that is intended to create a sense of action.

   ____

7. Underline the word that best describes Harley:

   careless   neglectful   self-confident   cruel

EXERCISE H

(answer page 174)

Using the numbers 1 to 5, list these events in the order they occurred for Harley.

_______ Harley gets a slippery-dip to play on.

_______ Harley is given a new bike.

_______ Harley plays ball with Podgy.

_______ Harley overfeeds the goldfish.

_______ Harley has his first day at school.

EXERCISE I

(answer page 174)

Find the meanings of these words as used in the story.

experiences: ______________________________

____

U-turn: ______________________________

____

cradled: ______________________________

____

looming: ______________________________

____

yanked: ______________________________

____

EXERCISE J

(answer page 174)

What feeling or emotion is being suggested by the following sentences taken from the story?

1. Harley's mom could hardly keep her mouth from dropping open. ______________
2. Harley's mom gave a long sigh. ______________
3. "Take off the training wheels, Dad," he said. "I don't need them." ______________
4. He [Harley] was too busy ruffling Podgy's ears. ______________
5. "Is everything alright?" she [Harley's mother] begged. ______________

EXERCISE K

(answer page 174)

List three words that author has used that are more expressive than *said*.

______________ ______________ ______________

EXERCISE L

(answer page 174)

1. What plays the more important role in this narrative? (Underline one.)

   descriptions　　　events

2. The first day at school has changed Harley. How has his attitude changed?

3. What action does Harley take that shows a change has taken place?

4. Harley's first day at school changed his parents. How have Harley's parents changed?

5. The clause "Harley ended up in a tangle of bicycle on the pansy garden" creates a word picture. Briefly explain the picture you imagine.

30 Using Metaphors, Similes, and Clichés

In class, you may have been told about metaphors, similes, and clichés.

Here's a quick reminder.

A **simile** is when we say something is similar to something else. For example:

After a mouthful of hot curry, Angus roared **like a bull**.

A **metaphor** is when we identify something in terms of another object. For example:

Angus climbed **the hill of life** without too many problems.

A **cliché** is an expression that has been overused/overworked. Try to avoid them! Examples:

The rain **came down in buckets**. It was as **cold as ice**.

Writing Tip

Metaphors and similes are two of the main tools of figurative language. They should be used with care. Too many can be off-putting for the reader or make the writing trite and commonplace!

(answer page 174)

Highlight the similes in this short passage.

Although the blossoms were as red as blood now, by nightfall they would be like used bandages. Craig wondered if he should have bought plastic flowers. At least they didn't curl up and wilt like cotton candy in the hot sun. Trouble was they looked as phoney as the set of a school play.

(answer page 174)

Highlight the metaphors in this passage.

Joan's bedroom was a pigsty. In a far corner was a pile of dirty clothes waiting to do battle with any individual who might even consider removing them to the laundry. The hastily discarded school exercise books made a variety of badly built pyramids on her desk. The lonely ceiling light watched with disinterest.

Single-Word Metaphors

Sometimes a single word can act as a metaphor. In the above example *lonely* is a single-word metaphor.

Consider the effect of the **bold** words in these sentences.

The car **sailed** down the motorway. (We know that cars don't sail.)

The staff tried to **hammer** out a solution to the problem of overcrowding.

It was a **sad** little stream that **struggled** through the litter left by visitors.

EXERCISE C

(answer page 174)

Highlight one word in the parentheses that creates a metaphor for each of these sentences.

1. Good exam results are a (guide, door, clue) to future success.
2. The (long, many, cruel) years of toil made the farmer look and feel old.
3. One of the workers was a bull and the other was a (weakling, foreman, lamb).

EXERCISE D

(answer page 174)

Complete these sentences with a one-word metaphor.

1. The beaten dog (verb) ____________________ its way through the crowd to the scrub.

2. The new seedlings wilted (adverb) ____________________ in the dry sunshine.

Warning!

Don't mix metaphors. They can sound ludicrous. For example:

After giving the coach a piece of his mind, he realized he had burned his bridges.

To succeed you must keep your nose to the grindstone and your head held high.

EXERCISE E

(answer page 174)

Similes can improve writing, but they must be appropriate. For example, in a ghost story we might write: Abandoned spiders' webs hung from the beams like the threads of a torn shroud.

Which is the most appropriate simile for a pirate story? Underline it.

She entered the cabin that was as clean as a new computer.

She entered the cabin that was as clean as a storm-washed drain.

She entered the cabin that was as clean as a beach on a desert island.

EXERCISE F

(answer page 174)

Add similes to this beginning to create three different impressions in the reader's mind.

Darren put the clock in his bag as if it were ____

Darren put the clock in his bag as if it were ____

Darren put the clock in his bag as if it were ____

Writing Tip

Similes do not always have to be at the end of the sentence. For example:

Like a flock of sheep the clouds filled the sky.

EXERCISE G

(answer page 174)

Suggest alternative similes, in the spaces, to the similes in this short passage.

The parade was about to start.

Ken stood as still as a toy soldier (_________________________________). His arms were as stiff as steel rods (_________________________________) and his head was held high like a guard on duty (_________________________________), but his heart sounded like waves on rocks after a storm (_________________________________).

EXTENSION

Here is a **sustained metaphor**. It is an image that is carried on for more than one sentence. In this example the metaphor is carried on for several lines of the poem.

> The train is a dragon that roars in the dark,
> It wriggles its tail and sends up a spark.
> It pierces the night with its one yellow eye,
> And all the world trembles as it rushes by.

EXERCISE H

(answer page 174)

1. What is the dragon's tail? ____________________

2. What is the dragon's roar? ____________________

3. Write your own poem using a sustained metaphor, modeled on the previous page. Here are some suggested subjects: sports car, hot air balloon, glider, submarine.

EXERCISE I

(answer page 174)

Below are some clichés. Give a brief meaning of the words in bold.

1. The seventh grade boys were **as thick as thieves**. ____________

2. The old man would be **turning in his grave**. ____________

3. Marianne was **skating on thin ice**. ____________

4. For Grandma **the sands of time were running out**. ____________

5. By **burning the midnight oil** Sally completed her essays. ____________

Writing Tip

Often the actual meaning will be more effective than the cliché.

EXERCISE J

Write a brief description of a sporting match using some metaphors and similes.

31 Adding Impact with Personification and Hyperbole

Personification

Personification means giving **human characteristics** to non-human things. It is usually done using verbs, adjectives, and adverbs. For example:

The brooding trees watched the children lost in the forest.

Trees don't brood or watch. That is something people do.

Exercise A

(answer page 175)

Highlight (or underline) the examples of personification in these sentences.

1. The angry sea raged against the stubborn rocks.
2. Vines grabbed at Yuri's legs as he stumbled down the steep hillside.

Hyperbole

Hyperbole (hi-perb-olly) means using **exaggeration for effect**. For example:

I've told you a million times not to call me "dearie."

There is no way that someone would say that a million times, but the reader gets the message—it has been said many, many times.

Exercise B

(answer page 175)

Highlight (or underline) the examples of hyperbole in these sentences.

1. The chili sauce was so hot it left a cinder trail down his throat.
2. Men of iron withstood the never-ending attack of enemy troops.

Exercise C

(answer page 175)

Compare these two paragraphs about the same subject.

Passage 1

After gushing from the snowfields of the distant mountains, the slow-flowing stream eddied by mossy rocks towards the distant reed-filled pool of stagnant water. This was its final destination. Here the water would collect in spring and then slowly evaporate during the hot summer.

Passage 2

After bounding restlessly from the snowfields of the distant mountains, the sad little stream crawled by mossy rocks towards the solemn, reed-filled pool of stagnant water. This was its final place of rest. Here the sleepy water would collect in spring and then lazily evaporate during the blistering summer.

1. Which passage makes greater use of personification? ________________________________

2. Which example of personification do you think is most effective? ________________________

EXERCISE D

(answer page 175)

Using the letter **p** (for personification) and **h** (for hyperbole) identify the techniques used in these sentences.

1. I waited a thousand years for the bus to come. _______

2. The teacher made her way through the mountain of books on her desk. _______

3. The sun smiled on the holiday makers for a whole week. _______

4. The streetlights were watchful eyes along the road. _______

5. We could hear a pin drop during the service. _______

6. A bare and empty table waited in the dark kitchen. _______

EXERCISE E

(answer page 175)

Read this passage. Hyperbole and personification are used to amuse the reader.

At seven-thirty each night the horror begins. Freddie has to go to bed.

He has to travel down the dark hall to the bathroom to have his bath. Then he must brush his teeth in the steaming, spooky jungle of pipes and plants where the gas heater wheezes warnings of doom. He has to go to the toilet too, which is out on the back veranda—out there where the mango tree hangs over the whole garden like a black umbrella.

If he has survived this far, Fred must then creep down the darker-than-ever hall to his bedroom. His terrible bedroom, fairly swarming with goblins, ogres, zombies, and things. He must climb into bed by the safest possible route and pull the covers over his head and hide until morning.

From: *Freddie the Frightened* by Pamela Shrapnel

1. Give an example of hyperbole from the passage. ________________________________

2. Give an example of personification from the passage. ____________________________

EXERCISE F

Check some humorous books in your library to find examples of personification and hyperbole.

Write the titles here: ____________________

EXERCISE G

Using hyperbole, write a sentence or two about this cartoon.

EXERCISE H

Write a few fictional lines about your worst (or best) day at school, using examples of personification and hyperbole. You may also include metaphors and similes.

EXERCISE I

(answer page 175)

Highlight any examples of personification or hyperbole you can find in this passage.

My dad is the biggest liar in the whole world. When I was at the bottom of the class in math, he told his friends that I was very close to the top. He can't live with the notion that his only child cannot do a single math question. It makes him madder than an angry bull-ant. All the bull-ants I have come across know more math than I do!

My dad's the local garbage truck driver–and that's the problem. He wants me to have a good education so that I can earn a million dollars before I'm twenty-five. No chance. Even if I did, he'd want me to spend half of it on his sorry old truck. Half the time it's so sick it cannot get up enough enthusiasm to carry an idea half way down our street.

I've been waiting for years for you to return my call.
Your excuses are as old as the pyramids. I've been wading through mountains of paper to get the information!

32 Using Different Text Types

Text types are the different ways people present the written word. A newspaper report is quite different from a film review or a poster.

In many stories, using different text types can add variety to your story telling, highlight a particular point, and allow you to avoid long descriptions. For example, when I found it difficult to describe a fictional school burning down, I made up a **newspaper report** to record the event. I have never seen a school burn down. The report in the paper let me record the frightening event without the detail. In another case a **business card** allowed me to give a quick rundown on a situation.

Exercise A

(answer page 175)

Look at this business card and note how quickly it gives a lot of information.

From information on the card, what four things might you say about this business?

1. ______________________________

2. ______________________________

3. ______________________________

4. ______________________________

Exercise B

This is a list of some of the text types used when writing fiction. Place a checkmark by any you have recently used.

Newspaper reports
Business cards
Fliers
Posters
Play reviews
Emails
Faxes
Historical records
Comic strips
Cartoons
Diaries

Maps
Sets of rules
Instructions
Sketches
Advertisements
Letters
Programs
Classified ads
Timetables
Editorials

Memos
Drama scripts
Recorded messages
Postcards
Storefront signs
Graffiti
Words of a song
Poetry
Photographs
Recipes

Examples

Different text types also allow the reader to bring different information to your story.

In the story *My Sad Skeleton*, I used a flier (notice) similar to this one. It was found in the family letterbox.

This flier allowed me to give a lot of information and impressions of the fair without going into lengthy detail. It also allowed the reader to use his or her imagination.

Using different text types is not new. In *Treasure Island*, Robert Louis Stevenson uses the words of a song, a letter, and a map.

EXERCISE C

(answer page 175)

1. To which group of people do you think the poster would appeal? ____________________

2. What is your reaction to some of the attractions? ____________________

____

3. Why is the word *much* repeated so often? ____________________

EXERCISE D

(answer page 175)

Read this extract from a historical magazine, which provided me some background information for *Aitutaki Phantom* without going into lengthy detail.

The Flying Boat Era

After the war, many air services to South Pacific destinations began. Huge flying boats flew across the Pacific with the Aitutaki Lagoon being a destination, as well as a safe haven.

The Sandringhams were not the typical four engine "flying boats." Over 30 tons in weight, these carried 50 passengers on two decks.

They provided meals cooked by the stewardesses.

Sandringhams often flew less than 1,000 meters above sea level and could take over a minute to get airborne off a watery runway.

They landed near Akaimi Inlet and were refuelled by hand using dozens of oil drums.

On one trip an engine died on take-off . . .

How would you describe the above article? ____________________

____

EXERCISE E

(answer page 175)

1. In Chapter 6 of *Harry Potter and the Sorcerer's Stone* by J.K. Rowling, Harry finds a card inside a chocolate frog wrapper. What sort of card was it? Highlight one.

   sports card witch/wizard card free frog card magic trick instructions

2. What different text type is used in Chapter 13 of *Charlotte's Web* by E.B. White?

____

(*Note:* If you cannot find copies of these books, look in some other books for different text types.)

1. Create a flier (mailbox notice) for a fictitious event to be held in your local community. The event, organized by the school, is called *Saturday's Super Skateboard Sizzler.*

2. Create a front yard sign for a spooky house for sale.

Developing a "What if?" element 33

What is "What if?" in story writing?

In simple terms it is something that adds another level, complication, or problem to your story idea. For example, you might want to write a story about a football team getting a new coach for the season. The team is desperate to win. You have some good ideas about some of the things that will happen in your story. You want to add more tension to your story. What if the new coach was a woman?

Try another example. You want to rewrite the fairy tale *The Three Little Pigs*. You want to make your story really interesting. What if the pigs all live in a big city? Fiona French rewrote the Snow White story as *Snow White in New York*.

Writing Tip

The "What if?" can relate to a **person**, as in the first example above, to a change of **place**, as in the suggestion above for *The Three Little Pigs*, or to a change of **time**. What if *The Three Little Pigs* happens in the future?

My story *So Much for Aliens* was a rewrite of the Indian story of six blind men and the elephant. What if the blind men were sightless space visitors and the elephant was an abandoned car?

EXERCISE A

(answer page 175)

This is the start of a changed, simplified fable. Can you recognize it?

> A long time ago a stray cat was prowling the city streets looking for food. It came to a deserted house with the front door open. The cat went inside in its search for food. A sudden gust of wind blew the door shut. The cat was trapped in the dark house and would die if it couldn't escape. It started crying for help.
>
> A mouse was living in the house. It called from the safety of its hole to find out what was distressing the cat.
>
> The cat explained that it would die if it didn't get out. The mouse said it could help.
>
> The cat laughed at this idea. How could a little mouse help a trapped cat? Didn't the mouse know that cats ate mice?
>
> But the mouse knew how to release a special bolt on the outside of a cat flap. The mouse could go through its hole in the wall and free the cat.

1. What was the original fable? ______________________________

2. The original fable was set in the jungle. Where is this version set? ______________________________

3. What was the stray cat in the original version of the fable? ______________________________

4. How was the animal in the original version trapped? ______________________________

EXERCISE B

(answer page 175)

Take these well-known stories and suggest a change in character, place, or time. For example:

Snow White and the Seven Dwarfes. What if the dwarfes are not dwarfes but performers in a traveling circus?

If you are unfamiliar with a suggested story, replace it with one you know.

1. *Brer Rabbit and the Tar Baby*. What if ______________________________

2. *Little Red Riding Hood*. What if ______________________________

3. *Robinson Crusoe*. What if ______________________________

4. *Town Mouse and Country Mouse*. What if ______________________________

5. *Treasure Island*. What if ______________________________

6. *The Ant and the Grasshopper* (Aesop fable). What if ______________________________

7. *The Little Red Engine*. What if ______________________________

8. *Robin Hood*. What if ______________________________

EXERCISE C

What if
Cinderella was
a fella?

Select two stories you know and have a "What if?" for character, place, and time.

Story 1: ______________________________

What if (character) ______________________________

What if (place) ______________________________

What if (time) ______________________________

What if Alice's Wonderland was on another planet?

Story 2: ______________________________

What if (character) ______________________________

What if (place) ______________________________

What if (time) ______________________________

What if Tarzan lived in the next century?

EXERCISE D

Select a story you are familiar with and start a rewrite of that story with a change of place, time, or character or a combination of these.

Original title: ______________________________

New title: ______________________________

34 Creating Atmosphere

What is atmosphere in story writing? Simply put, it is the mood or feelings a story (or film) creates in the reader's mind.

(answer page 176)

Read these two examples of the same incident: "A Walk in the Forest."

Example 1

It was a mild autumn day. A soft breeze blew through buttercup yellow and ruby red leaves of protective forest trees. Fallen leaves bounced and danced across the trail as Andy wandered happily towards the sparkling brook. Soon the first glistening crystals of snow would blanket the sleeping earth.

Example 2

It was a gray autumn day. A gusty wind whipped through the sickly yellow and blood red leaves of the threatening forest giants. Discarded leaves careened angrily across the rough track as Andy struggled towards the sluggish stream. Soon the first onslaught of chilling snow would smother the dying earth.

Which example is more likely to be from a romance story? __________

The examples should have drawn different word pictures in your imagination, yet they both describe a similar incident.

EXERCISE B

(answer page 176)

Add adjectives to the following sentences to change the atmosphere as indicated in the parentheses. The first is done for you.

Two men in **dark** clothes stood watching the **troubled** crowd. (suspense)

Two men in ____________ clothes stood watching the ____________ crowd. (doom)

Two men in ____________ clothes stood watching the ____________ crowd. (anticipation)

EXERCISE C

(answer page 176)

Similes can also help create atmosphere in your stories. Add a simile to these sentences to compliment the subject of the story. The first is done for you.

1. Desert quest: The afternoon sun dried their lips **like the leaves on a stunted shrub**.
2. Space adventure: Anders tip-touched the wall. It was as hot ______________________________
3. Horror: His cape flew out behind him like ______________________________
4. Pirate story: A bough fell from an old tree making a crack like ______________________________
5. Sport: Alan jumped into the air as if he were ______________________________
6. Fairy tale: The men sat huddled under the umbrella like ______________________________
7. Fable: The hare saw the hunter sneaking through the forest like ______________________________

Writing Tip

The exercises above focused on adjectives and similes. Verbs, adverbs, and metaphors can also help create atmosphere. For example: The silent moon watched tirelessly as the attack team prowled stealthily across the shadowy space like tigers on the hunt.

EXERCISE D

(answer page 176)

Draw lines to match the type of story with the sentence.

Sentence	Type
Many years ago a cunning fox tried to outsmart a wise old owl.	western
The tomb-like room was full of shadows swirling like gray mist.	fantasy
The kitchen stool was harder than any saddle and just about as high.	fable
The fairy landed on Dana's outstretched arm with a soft flutter.	horror

EXERCISE E

(answer page 176)

Read this passage and then choose the atmosphere it best depicts.

> The track seemed to peter out altogether.
>
> Shane was undecided as to whether he should continue down the gully or simply retrace his steps. Suddenly, he was aware of how quiet the wild was. It was an uncanny quiet.
>
> The fleeting thought of seeing a kangaroo crossed his mind. It didn't look like kangaroo country–whatever that was. He looked around nervously, not sure what he expected to see.
>
> Nothing moved. The stunted white-barked gums looked strangely ominous. Dead branches, like bony fingers and arms, reached to the sky for help that would not come. Growth abnormalities on the trunks looked like the distorted faces of deformed gargoyles.
>
> From: *Cadaver Dog*

1. The passage creates a feeling of:

   excitement menace isolation anticipation success

2. What does the sentence "The stunted white-barked gums look strangely ominous" make you think of?

   ____

3. What is a gargoyle? ______________________________

RESEARCH

Find a book or story that creates each of the following feelings:

peacefulness: ______________________________

loneliness: ______________________________

fear: ______________________________

companionship: ______________________________

suspense: ______________________________

pride: ______________________________

perseverance: ______________________________

doom: ______________________________

Writing Tip

Don't try to maintain the same atmosphere for the whole of your story. Too much of anything becomes tiresome. Even in his darkest tragedies Shakespeare used some comic relief.

EXERCISE F

Write a short passage that is intended to make the reader feel contented or satisfied.

Suggested topics: a day on a tropical beach, a family outing, finishing a difficult task, the end of the school year

EXERCISE G

(answer page 176)

This passage from *Sounder* by William H. Armstrong creates a feeling of isolation and hopelessness. Highlight four terms that contribute to creating those feelings.

> No dim lights from the other cabins punctuated the night. The white man who owned the vast endless fields had scattered cabins of his sharecroppers far apart like flyspecks on a whitewashed ceiling. Sometimes on Sundays the boys walked with their parents to set awhile at one of the distant cabins. Sometimes they went to the meetin' house. And there was school too. But it was far away at the edge of town. Its term began after harvest and ended before planting time. Two successive Octobers the boys had started walking the eight miles mornings and evenings.

35 Starting a "Good Word" List

Many writers make a point of keeping a record of interesting and exciting words that they find. These are not necessarily new words but words they have more or less forgotten or don't use in everyday conversation.

Here are three interesting words I found and made use of.

judder: It means to shake or vibrate as a train might do when it starts rolling. (It's probably a mixture of *jar* and *shudder*.)

raddled: It means to have an unkempt (untidy) and run-down appearance.

feisty: It carries a sense of assertiveness and aggressiveness with it. Someone described a young girl in one of his stories as feisty.

In this space, keep a list of words that may come in useful later on. It may be wise to give brief definitions or show how they are used.

Here is a short story. Read it and then look for examples of writing techniques that have been used.

Friend for Penny

"A dog? For me?" said Penny.

"It is your birthday next Sunday," said her father. "We should get it now."

"Then you'll have it for your birthday," explained her mother. "We don't want to start looking on your birthday. What sort of dog would you like?"

"Just a dog that'll be a friend," smiled Penny.

"Not a dog that digs up gardens," warned her mother.

"We can look in the paper now," said her father. He opened the paper and found:

DOGS FOR SALE

Penny saw her father's smile turn to a frown as he read.

"What's wrong?" asked Penny.

"Well, they all seem very expensive," replied her father.

"Let me see," said her mother.

She looked down the column of dogs for sale. "These are all special dogs. They cost too much for us!"

Penny felt sad.

Her mother folded the paper. "What do we do now?"

"Hey, let's look in the pet shop!" suggested Penny. "There's a new one at the shopping mall."

Her parents thought that was a sensible idea.

They all climbed into their car and went to the pet store.

From the parking lot they saw the pet store. Balloons and streamers covered the window.

Inside the store there were birds in cages, rabbits eating carrots, and fish in fish tanks. There were fluffy kittens in baskets that Penny softly stroked as she looked about.

There weren't many dogs.

A poodle called Fifi had a pink blob of curly hair on the end of her tail.

"I don't want a poodle," Penny said. "Its tail is like a pom-pom. I'd have to dye its hair and keep giving it haircuts!"

"What about the chihuahua?" asked her mother.

"It's like . . . a big rat!" said Penny. "Our cat would chase it."

People in the shop laughed.

Penny said, "I just want a dog that'll be a friend."

The store-owner said, "Why not go to the dog fair? Lots of different dogs at the fair."

"What a good idea," agreed Penny's mother.

"There's one in the park today," said the store-owner. "It's like a picnic fun day for dogs and their owners."

Arriving at the park they saw lots of dogs with their proud owners.

There were tall dogs and hairy dogs. Dogs catching frisbees.

Penny's father said, "Let's talk to the people about their dogs."

The first lady they met had a dog walking on its back legs.

"This is Tricksy," she said. "She does tricks."

'"That's my dog, Tiger," said a man. "Look, he can jump over small fences. He can jump through hoops!"

"This is Tarzan," said the next person. "He can fetch sticks. And the Sunday paper."

There were dogs that could shake hands.

Dogs that could walk on big balls.

Penny said, "I don't want a dog that does silly tricks. I just want a dog that'll be a friend."

"I don't know where to try now," said her mother.

Slowly selecting his words her father suggested, "There is one place we could try."

"Where?" asked Penny and her mother.

"We could try the pound."

"The pound! That's full of dogs people don't want!" they both cried.

Then Penny's mother said, "You never know."

As they drove to the pound, Penny felt disappointed.

When they got out of the car, they could hear dogs barking. Penny didn't want to go in.

No one said much as they walked up and down between the dog cages.

They saw hairy dogs and dogs with long legs.

Dogs with litters of puppies.

And dogs that just barked and barked.

Penny put her hands over her ears and walked to the end of the path.

In the cage next to her was a black dog with white patches.

It wasn't barking. It just looked at her.

"You're scruffy!" growled Penny.

The dog lifted one ear and looked at her.

Penny started to walk off.

She looked back at the scruffy dog.

The dog wagged its tail–just a little.

Just then her parents joined her.

"What do you think?" asked her father. "The vet here says this dog is good with children."

"It's scruffy!" declared Penny. "But I suppose we could give him a good wash and comb his hair."

"What could you call him?" asked her father.

"I don't like fancy dogs–or fancy names. I really want a friend," explained Penny.

Her parents waited.

The dog put its head to one side.

"And he is so scruffy," said Penny. "That's what he'll be! Scruffy! Let's go home, Scruffy."

And Scruffy went home with Penny and her parents.

Scruffy and Penny quickly became good friends.

EXERCISE A

(answer page 176)

Respond to the following.

1. Find an example of repetition of a phrase or sentence: ______________________________

2. What text type, other than narrative, is used in the story? ______________________________

3. Find an example of the use of the sense of hearing. ______________________________

4. Find an example of the use of the sense of touch. ______________________________

5. Find an example of a simile. ______________________________

6. Make a comment about the title. ______________________________

7. Make a comment about the coda. ______________________________

8. List four words used instead of *said*. ______________________________

9. How would you describe the father? ______________________________

10. What words/actions helped you draw this conclusion? ______________________________

____

11. How would you describe Penny? ______________________________

12. What words/actions helped you draw this conclusion? ______________________________

____

13. In your opinion, is Penny a suitable name for the daughter? ______________________________

14. Give two examples of concrete detail. ______________________________

15. Find an example of an incomplete sentence. ______________________________

16. Find an example of a verb beginning a sentence. ______________________________

17. Find an example of an adverb beginning a sentence. ______________________________

18. What is the problem that is solved in the story? ______________________________

19. Give one example of an attempt to solve the problem. ______________________________

20. How does Penny's attitude change as the family go from one place to another?

____

37 Responding to a Prompt

In many of the exercises given in schools (and some competitions), the writer has to respond to a given prompt. In other words, the writer has to start cold with another person's idea.

The prompt can take a number of forms: a title, a first sentence, a last sentence, a graphic, a theme. Sometimes there may be a choice.

A Recommended Approach

1. Give yourself some thinking time (time to reflect on the topic/prompt).
2. Jot down as many ideas as you can (personal brainstorming). It doesn't matter if the ideas seem silly at first. It will be easier later to discard them than to try and recall them.
3. Be familiar with the basic structure of a story.
4. Imagine some characters (who) and settings (where/when).
5. Add a "What if?" or two.
6. Jot down some concrete ideas that relate to the topic.
7. Check your ideas books. You might have an idea that can be readily adapted.
8. Isolate a problem that can be associated with the topic/prompt.
9. Write a simple outline. This can be changed as your ideas begin to flow.
10. Start writing even if you feel a little uncertain. That's when the ideas will start to flow and the imagination will free itself from the pressures of the task. In your first draft, don't worry about making mistakes.

Exercise A

If you are given a theme, jot down any ideas that quickly come into your head. Here is an example:

Theme: "Congratulations"

Ideas: winning a race, a sporting match, a lottery, a school prize, 100th birthday, getting a new brother/sister, a literary/art competition, first person on Mars, court case, getting married/divorced, a negative congrats for doing something foolish (getting a weird job, making an embarrassing mistake), mixed-up ceremony, wrong winner, kicking a goal for the opposition

Now quickly jot down some ideas for the themes below and on page 153.

Theme: "Afraid"

Ideas: ____

____

____

Theme: "Lost"

Ideas: ______________________________

EXERCISE B

Here is an example of ideas prompted by a graphic:

> **Ideas:** breaking into my room, stealing, flowers, money, keys, robber is un/known, robber is a learner, a bungler, a female
>
> What if? robber is Dad breaking into school to get my essay that gives away family secrets/my diary, wrong school

Now jot down some ideas for stories prompted by this graphic.

Ideas: ______________________________

EXERCISE C

You may be given the first line of a story and asked to write the next few paragraphs. For example, the sentence might be:

> "Joanna walked into her room and immediately noticed something was missing or out of place."

Ideas and thoughts:

What's missing? Money, wallet, love letters, books, goldfish . . .

Out of place? Drawers not shut, objects on dressing table moved . . .

Window open, cat under bed, footprints, strange smell

Light bulb removed

Joanna walked into her room and immediately noticed something was missing or out of place.

Hardly touching her treasures, she checked the items on her dressing table, one by one.

Her favorite pen was exactly where she had left it. Her hairbrush was sitting neatly by her pink comb.

She turned to her window. It was slightly, ever so slightly open at the bottom–and her pot of pink African violets was not on the window sill!

Now, it is your turn. Jot down your ideas in the ideas box and write the first paragraph or two of a story that starts with: "Uncle Lambert arrived on Friday the thirteenth."

Ideas and thoughts:

Uncle Lambert arrived on Friday the thirteenth. ______________________________

EXERCISE D

You are given this title: *Dodgem-car Disaster*

Ideas and thoughts:

Write the first few paragraphs of the story.

Write a brief outline here.

EXERCISE E

You are asked to write a story that ends with this line:

"It's the only cat I've ever seen at a dog show."

Ideas and thoughts:

Write the first few paragraphs of the story.

Write a brief outline here.

List below eight of the stories you have written. Then use the checklist on the next page to see how many of the features described in this guide you have used in your stories. Remember, it is not necessary to incorporate all the features explained in this guide to have a successful story. In fact, it may not be beneficial to good story writing.

1. ______________________________
2. ______________________________
3. ______________________________
4. ______________________________
5. ______________________________
6. ______________________________
7. ______________________________
8. ______________________________

Things to think about for future stories:

CHECKLIST FOR STORY WRITING

Feature	Your Story							
	1	2	3	4	5	6	7	8
Title selected								
Use of concrete detail								
Opening paragraph(s)								
Closing paragraph(s)								
Variety in sentence types								
Variety in sentence lengths								
Variety in sentence beginnings								
Repetition								
Use of the senses—sight								
Use of the senses—hearing								
Use of the senses—touch								
Use of the senses—smell								
Use of the senses—taste								
Use of direct/indirect speech								
Character characteristics								
Showing, not telling								
Consistent point of view								
Use of *said, look,* and *went* words								
Developed story structure/climax								
Use of metaphors or similes								
Use of personification or hyperbole								
Use of different text types								
"What if" factor incorporated								
Atmosphere developed								
Some new/unusual words used								

1. To become a competent writer, you need to practice. The more you practice, the better you will become (just like a golfer or swimmer).
2. Enter your work in competitions. Competitions have guidelines that will make you look more critically at your efforts.
3. Don't be afraid of not getting it right first attempt. All authors have rewritten pages of their work because the first try didn't sound right.
4. Keep a notebook for ideas ever handy. Write your ideas down no matter how silly they might sound at the time. Who would have thought stories about a talking spider or pig (*Charlotte's Web*, *Babe*) would make a million dollars? The Paddington Bear books started with a very simple idea.
5. Read a variety of books/authors on the subject matter that interests you as a writer. Maybe someone has already written a similar story. Maybe you can write a better version of the story.
6. Don't forget that personal experiences are an important source of information.
7. When you are writing and the story seems to want to jump from your brain to the page don't worry about spelling, grammar, capital letters, and such. If you are "on a roll," they can be corrected later.
8. Don't worry about starting with a title. It will pop into your head later.
9. Make sure you have a dictionary and a thesaurus handy.
10. Don't be afraid of criticism (revisions can be made).
11. Listen to authors talking about their writing experiences. Many schools have visiting authors and writing workshops.
12. Let the imagination run free.

FICTION BOOKS BY ALAN HORSFIELD

So Much for Aliens, Thomson Nelson (Buzz Words series 1), 1996.

Age Level: Mid-primary Setting: Wild land

Science fiction/humor. Old Sam tells Josh about some aliens in the wild. When Josh investigates, he finds the aliens very confused about a discovery they have made.

The Big Race, Thomson Nelson (Buzz Words series 2), 1997.

Age Level: Mid-primary Setting: School sports

Miles wants to win the school cross-country race, but he has some stiff competition from "Claws" Magee.

"Lemming Run" in *Then and Now*, Wannabee Publishing, 1997.

Age Level: Young adult/adult Setting: City to surf

The Sydney City to Surf Fun Run is reported from a child's veiwpoint. The impression created is one of a prisoner of war march.

The Ghost Writer, Macmillan Educational (Crackers series), 1997.

Age Level: Upper-primary, lower secondary Setting: Suburban

Mystery and suspense. When Michael discovers a wanted ad for a ghost writer for a voodoo experience, he applies and gets the job, not realizing that he will become another victim in an evil scheme.

Monopillar, Thomson Nelson Educational (Blitzit series), 1997.

Age Level: Mid/Upper-primary Setting: Sydney, Darling Harbor

Science fiction. Jason discovers that one of the monorail trains is really a metallic caterpillar, kept alive by some evil museum scientists. After metamorphosis, it is a giant spaceship.

Bubble Buster, Blake Education (Sparklers series), 1998

Age Level: Lower-primary Setting: Suburban

Fantasy. Buster has an adventure over the city trapped in a huge bubble.

Aitutaki Phantom, Nelson ITP, 1999

Age Level: Mid/Upper-primary Setting: Cook Islands

Time-warp adventure. While on vacation on Aitutaki Island, Aaron discovers a flying boat has made an emergency landing on the lagoon. Flying boats have not landed at Aitutaki for more than fifty years.

My Sad Skeleton, Wendy Pye NZ (Galaxy Kids series), 2002.

Age Level: Lower-primary Setting: Suburban

Fantasy/humor. Jed's father keeps a skeleton in a box. When Jed opens the box, he finds a sad, lonely skeleton. Jed sets about finding ways to make the skeleton happy.

The Strange Story of Elmer Floyd, Longman Pearson (Just Kids series), 2002.

Age Level: Lower-primary Setting: Suburban

Humorous adventure. Elmer watches too much television. Later, he has a problem separating fact from fiction.

Daily Bread, Blake Education (Gigglers series), 2002.

Age Level: Lower-primary Setting: Home

Humorous family situation. Mom gets a new breadmaker, but her experiments embarass her children.

"Dream on, Brian" in children's stories collection *Dreams*, Ginninderra Press, 2002.

Age Level: Lower-primary Setting: Home

Humorous family situation. Brian likes to daydream, but his daydreaming gets him into trouble.

The Brahmin and the Ungrateful Tiger, Nelson ITP, 2003.

Age Level: Mid-primary Setting: India

Retold folktale. A Brahmin releases a tiger from a cage only to become a possible meal for the tiger.

The Rats of Wolfe Island, Lothian, 2002 (young adult fiction)

Age Level: Young adult Setting: Fiji Islands

Suspense adventure. On a remote Pacific Island, Eddie comes across a scientist doing experiments on rats exposed to atomic radiation. The experiments have unexpected results.

Dr. awKwarD, Macmillan NZ, 2003.

Age Level: Upper-primary Setting: Suburban

Mystery, humorous adventure. Dr. awKwarD is a rock-and-roll has-been. When his latest hit is ridiculed by a DJ, he decides to take revenge on society by jumbling sounds. Hannah finds a way to frustrate his evil scheme by using palindromes.

Cadaver Dog, Lothian (Crime Waves mystery), 2003.

Age Level: Lower-primary Setting: Australian wild

Mystery, suspense. Shane and his father attempt to start a new life on the site of a closed school. The grounds have a past that is slowly revealed to Shane with the help of a sniffer dog.

Great Hair Robbery, Lothian (Start Up series), 2003 (also available as an audio book: Bolindo Audio 2003).

Age Level: Mid-primary Setting: Suburban

Nellie discovers that everyone has had their hair stolen. With the help of two inept detectives, she finds the thief.

NO Signs (picture book to be published by Peranga Post Press, 2004).

Age Level: Picture Book Setting: Suburban

David is dismayed by all the negative signs in the community and decides to do something about it.

****Extracts from a number of the above books have been used in this book.

1 WRITING FICTION (NARRATIVES) PAGES 7–10

Exercise A

Extract 1: recount; Extract 2: narrative

Exercise B

peeping, heavy, cloaked, downpour, scurrying, thrown, gaudy, waited, neglected

Exercise C

Example: It was Monday, the special Monday. After a hurried breakfast, we gathered excitedly on our front lawn and waited. We were waiting for our new car. The car Dad had won in the art contest . . .

Exercises D and E

Individual responses. Types of features you could highlight include incomplete sentences, atmosphere, figurative language, variation in sentence length, or direct speech.

3 WRITING WHAT YOU KNOW—FIRST-HAND EXPERIENCES PAGE 16

Exercise E

Internet, library, reference books, videos, magazines

Always Check Your Sources

possum: marsupial; squirrel: bushy tailed rodent

4 CHOOSING TITLES (WHAT'S IN A NAME?) PAGES 18–21

Exercise A

magical frog, fairytale, fantasy, young children

Exercise C

younger readers

Exercise F (suggestions)

Circus Caper, Floating to Doom, Buried Alive!, The Short Life of Frosty, Pulpit for Polly

5 KNOWING THE IMPORTANCE OF DETAIL—CONCRETE OR GENERAL? PAGES 22–24

Exercise A

suburb – Union, Kentucky, beach – Malibu, TV show – Survivor, tree – cedar, sport – golf, flower – African violet, juice – tomato, magazine – *TV Guide*, fruit – avocado

Exercise B

(2) Hiding the wrapped box of chocolates behind his back, Mark stole up to the front door.

Exercise C (suggestions)

1. The white poodle sat happily in the sloppy mud.
2. Petra strolled into the seafood cafe and ordered potato wedges with chili sauce.
3. Kelly lay on the top sheet of her bunk bed and listened to the weather report on her transistor radio.
4. Smart-Mart's parking lot had three refrigerated food vans waiting by the side delivery dock.

Exercise D

1. The teenage audience reacted to the rock band's version of "Silent Night" with cheering and stamping.
2. Small striped beetles were crawling on the cold meat set out for the family reunion picnic.
3. Leanne chomped into the apple pie with its big dollop of imitation cream and then gulped down an orange juice.
4. Bison wandered languidly over the dry hills in search of blades of desert grass.
5. The roar of a rebel tank in the next street had pedestrians hurrying for shelter.
6. Old Mr. Groves, in his winter overcoat, hesitated by the newest headstone and silently read the inscription dedicated to his wife.

6 Creating Evocative Opening Paragraphs Pages 26–28

Exercise A (suggestion)

Where is the narrator at this point in time?

Exercise B (suggestions)

What is the ad about? Where is the narrator? Who is reading the ad?

Exercise C (suggestions)

What can Matthew see? What is the red object?

Exercise D

stone

Exercise F

Kon became aware that something was going to happen. Everyone was looking at something just behind his back, not too far away. What could it be?

Slowly, he turned his sandy head.

Dee Song giggled.

An explosion, so loud and unexpected that Kon fell backwards off his bench seat onto the grass, his right hand taking the full force of his fall.

The kids laughed loudly.

Kon struggled to his feet, glared angrily at the group and then looked at his right hand. He had chewing gum stuck to it.

Dee Song raised her hand to cover her mouth.

7 Writing Closing Paragraphs Pages 30–32

Exercise A

1. They both have repetition or similar wording. (Some kids never learn.)
2. Buster "splashes" in the pool.

Exercise B

Inconsiderate, appreciative

Exercise C

"You'd never catch me kissing a yukky frog."/ "I should hope not," said her mother as she turned out the light.

Exercise D

Jacinta turned the last corner of the cave. She saw the oval of sunlight that meant freedom. She scrambled past the last few rotten and broken support beams. As she left the opening, she didn't bother to look back at the "Keep Out" sign.

8 Adding Closing Sentences (Codas) Pages 33–36

Exercise A

"Dream on, Brian!" should be highlighted.

Exercise B

1. satisfied; 2. amused

Exercise C

Life will never be the same again for the narrator.

Exercise D (suggestions)

1. The pigs never again talked to a wolf.
2. With the Joker in prison, Robin could once again enjoy his book of jokes.
3. And Goldilocks decided never to eat porridge again!
4. The tortoise lay down and took a long nap. It was his turn.
5. (individual choice)

Exercise E (suggestion)

Auntie Dawn would not have kept her thoughts to herself!

9 Using Different Sentence Types — Pages 37–40

Exercise A

1. statement; 2. exclamation; 3. command; 4. command; 5. question

Exercise B

two

Exercise C (some variations possible)

It works, it really works! I can hardly believe it. My invention is working. It has been running for more than three minutes and is still working. Scientists from all over the world will want to see it. They will be speechless. Newspaper reporters will come with their photographers to do feature articles on me. And what will I tell them? I will say this is the first fully automatic short story writer.

Exercise E

1. It is Saturday morning of the school holidays.
2. Two–statements and questions

Exercise F

1. Three
2. They are all the same.
3. Reinforces the ignorance/lack of comprehension of the people.

Exercise G

1. Over and over. Entombed under tons of sand.
2. despair

10 Explaining Rhetorical Questions — Pages 41–42

Exercise A

anxious, worried, tense

Exercise B

thoughtful, inquisitive, curious

Exercise C

frightened, perplexed, puzzled

Exercise D (suggestions)

1. Should he look down? 2. Was it for her?

Exercise E

. . . so why were all the shops shut? OR
. . . so why was a hearse parked near her home?

11 Using Variety in Sentence Length — Pages 43–46

Exercise A

Passage 2–Short sentences create greater suspense.

Exercise B (suggestions)

1. Craig found his pen but his book was not in his bag.
2. Behind the seat Nellie saw a bus ticket near a ten-cent coin.
3. The tree was covered in long slender leaves and a sprinkling of blue tropical flowers, which had carpeted the ground.

Exercise C

1. The clown dove through the flaming hoop. He would finish with a forward roll. The curled toe of his shoe caught the hoop. Suddenly his costume was on fire.
2. The castle was dark. Kate felt frightened as she peered into the gloom. Chains started to rattle at the bottom of the stone stairs.
3. There are several types of vehicles on the island. There is a small truck used to pick up cargo. There are several beat-up taxis to pick up stray tourists. There is also a noisy mini-bus.

Exercise D (suggestion)

Chrissy twirled the string bag round and round her extended hand as she headed towards the supermarket. It was Friday afternoon. She was looking forward to a long weekend. She and her friend, Tracey Goodman, had planned many exciting activities. Watching the late night horror movie. Eating pizza in her bedroom. Playing Tracey's latest CDs and talking privately.

The afternoon sun was low in the western sky. The wide main street of Brookville offered little protection from its warm rays. She didn't mind.

12 Using Variety in Sentence Beginnings Pages 47–50

Exercise A (suggestions)

1. In their silent hunt for prey, red foxes won't be stopped by fences.
2. Red foxes are not stopped by fences when hunting silently for prey.

Exercise B (suggestions)

1. All the girls wore black hats.
2. Buzzing mosquitoes annoyed the tourists.
3. Before the dance, Jane dyed her hair.
4. Tuesdays are always a problem for teachers.

Exercise C

Large: adjective; Aaron: proper noun; Suddenly: adverb; Then: preposition; But: conjunction

Exercise D

1. The.
2. (Suggestion) Coming up over a moon crater was the early morning sun. The captain of the spacecraft put on his space suit. Slowly but finally the task was completed, and he was fully suited for a moonwalk. There was a quick wink from the engineer for his chief as the airlock door opened. After the captain entered the airlock, the door hissed closed. The captain was now on his own.

Exercise E (suggestions)

1. While waiting in the bus shelter, Morris found a crossword to complete.
2. Chaos will be created with too many helpers in the kitchen.
3. Being the youngest, Fred had to have first go on the swing.
4. With knowledge and commonsense, Andy was able to repair the mower.

Exercise F

1. Andres had passed out.
2. tough, blue
3. eyes, groin, words, Andres

13 Using Repetition Pages 51–54

Exercise A (suggestions)

There were people, people, and more people everywhere we looked.
All winter winds, wild wind and cold winds blew in from the south.

Exercise B

1. One pace.
2. He has great difficulty in walking. OR He is determined.

Exercise D

1. Repetition of the word *flies* makes the reader think of many flies.
2. Repetition of the word *all* reinforces the idea that it was a long period of time.

Exercise F

1. Mud; 2. individual responses

Exercise G (suggestion)

Bright, blaring bugles blasted the balmy morning breeze.

Exercise H

1. triangular, teeth (other examples possible); 2. harshness, viciousness, terror, fear; 3. terrible, titanic, tiny

14 Using All the Senses—Introduction/What Do You See? Pages 55–58

Exercise A

sound, smell, touch, taste

Exercise B

hearing

Exercise D

hearing, smelling, feeling, seeing

Exercise E (suggestions)

warm stones, black stones, rumbling stones, salty stones; stinging rain, fresh rain, rattling rain, driving rain, thirst-quenching rain; rusty truck, silent truck, smoky truck, gritty truck

Exercise F

Two hungry dogs: the dogs are abandoned, uncared for; damp grass: it is morning; back door: the dogs are waiting for food; abandoned shed: shed is in the wild

Exercise G (suggestion)

1. Val caught a glimpse of the dark van through the hushed crowd. It was by a dying tree near a graffitied bus stop where some ragged locals squatted around a smelly fire. Acrid smoke curled up from a battered drum. 2. individual responses

Exercise H

chirping birds: hearing; scented envelope: smell; hot motor: feel; jangling chains: hearing; dazzling sun: sight; salty chips: taste; sweet coffee: taste; dry paint: feel

Exercise I (suggestions)

A brisk wind whipped through the autumn leaves of the stately poplars and across the wide street. A whistling policeman standing on a quiet corner caught a whiff of scattered garbage. Taking a folded tissue from his pant pocket, he covered his raw nose.

Exercise J (suggestions)

It was a dull morning when Jim found a tartan shirt on a blackened thornbush.

Exercise K

grass looked like a magic carpet; asparagus patch looked like a silver forest; web was decorated with tiny beads of water; like a delicate veil

15 Using All the Senses— What Do You Feel? Pages 59–62

Exercise A

Fiona made her way across the bare, damp boards of the chilly room. Patches of the floor were so smooth that once or twice she almost slipped. In spots there were dark, sticky stains, as if oil had partially dried on the floor. Finally, she reached the window. With her finger, she rubbed a lop-sided circle in the coating of frost and grime that covered the entire surface. Then, before putting her finger in her warm mouth, she rubbed it clean on the coarse fabric of her coat.

Exercise B (suggestions)

1. wet, soggy, damp, moist, dry; 2. hot, warm, lukewarm, cool, chilly, cold; 3. hard, firm, resilient, pliable, spongy, soft; 4. rough, coarse, textured, smooth, silky

Exercise C

1. individual responses; 2. (suggestions) sting of a bull ant; prick of a pin; itch of hives; tingle of cold fingers; vibrations of power tools

Exercise D

flexible: bendable, lithe; throbbing: pulsating, vibrating; tepid: lukewarm, warmish; jar: jolt, rattle

Exercise E

harrowing: distressing, upsetting; smart: feel a sharp stinging pain; stun: cause unconsciouness by a sudden blow; numb: deprived of feeling through cold or shock; tingle: a prickling, itching or stinging sensation; feverish: suffering from fever, having a high body temperature and racing pulse

Exercise G

The truck jerked gently as Dan changed up a gear. The open flat road lay before him. The huge engine gently ticking over produced a soft rhythm of sound and pleasant throbbing vibrations. The cabin was warm and the steering wheel comfortable to hold. He could have been in a giant cocoon or, better still, the cockpit of a jumbo jet. The ride was that smooth.

The road beneath his wheels hummed monotonously and even the occasional dip or road repair gave little more than a kindly lift. It was like a gentle pat on the buttocks. Dan checked his gauges. No problems there. He tapped the fuel indicator. The needle flickered for a moment, then became stationary. All was well.

Time for a bit of music, he thought, and pressed the start button on the CD player.

Exercise H (suggestions)

1. aches, pain, throbbing discomfort, awkwardness; 2. warm, comfortable, satisfied, relaxed

16 Using all the senses— What do you hear? Pages 63–66

Exercise A

When the laughter of the other campers finally ceased, Ken expected silence. He longed for silence. But instead of silence, the wilderness outside was full of strange sounds.

A bird's mournful cry could be heard in a nearby, whispering tree. The monotonous trickle of the creek was like the incessant arguing of a distant group of children. Then he isolated the buzzing and hissing of strange insects, the rustling in the dry grass just by the tent where he was to sleep. He even became aware of his own breathing.

Exercise B (suggestions)

babble, hush, gurgle, screech, melody

Exercise C

1. clomp, rat-a-tat-tat; 2. (suggestions) boing, beep, pop, toot, put-put

Exercise D (suggestions)

hiss of car tires on a wet road; drone of an aircraft; splutter of a motor; tinkle of piano keys; chimes of a clock

Exercise E (suggestions)

cheep, chirp, squeak, scream, screech; thunderclap, blast, crack, pop, snap

Exercise F

hiss: snake; yowl: cat; warble: magpie; mew: cat/seagull; honk: goose; trumpet: elephant; bleat: sheep; grunt: pig

Exercise G

whimper: snivel, blubber; tuneful: melodious, musical; rowdy: noisy, loud; titter: snicker, giggle; rant: rave, rage; claptrap: poppycock, humbug

Exercise H

1. cacophony: harsh sound, dissonance; tattoo: beating on a drum; bass: lowest male singing voice; yelp: a sharp shrill bark or cry; bay: a deep long howl; catcall: loud cry expressing disapproval, especially at a meeting; 2. small bell

Exercise J

Down in the darkened bedroom Penelope was peeping out of the bedclothes with Fred, listening to the tap, tap tapping as the Googyman's cane came closer and closer to the windowsill.

A storm was building up. Perfect Googyman condition, Fred had whispered. Just the weather he needs to finish zapping the window locks.

Tap, tap, tap. Penelope looked across at Fred's trembling head on the other side of the elephant skin boot. Tap, tap, tap, tap, tap, tap, tap, tap, tap!

A roll of thunder followed a crack of lightning across the house and almost through the room.

Exercise K (suggestions)

bubble, splat, hiss, whistle, sizzle, crackle

17 Using all the senses—What do you smell? Pages 67–71

Exercise A

(1) It gives a clear word picture of Julie's actions.

Exercise B

Randy sniffed once. Then he sniffed again. He looked around the bus shelter, nose held high like a hound trying to identify a scent. The fumes from the departed bus were upsetting but there was something else. It wasn't a foul smell. It was a pleasant aroma. It had a trace of a sharp perfume or scent that seemed to sting the inside of his nostrils.

Exercise C (suggestions)

1. someone being sick; 2. rotting meat; 3. fresh bread

Exercise D (suggestions)

fume, fragrance, stink, scent, whiff

Exercise E (suggestions)

smell, inhale, snoop, sneeze

Exercise F

1. wine; 2. wild fowl (pheasant)

Exercise G (suggestions)

1. smoky, strong, odorless, fruity, musky, spicy; 2. fragrant rose, rancid meat, spicy sauce, stale cheese, smoky bacon, fruity syrup

Exercise H (suggestions)

swamp: foul, putrid; pine needles: fragrant, scented

Exercise I

aroma: odor, fragrance; foul: stinking, nauseating; putrid: decomposed, fetid; waft: float, drift; bouquet: perfume, fragrance; whiff: hint, scent

Exercise J

nauseating: causing a feeling of needing to be sick/vomit; fusty: smelling of dampness or mold; noisome: offensive smell; deodorize: remove or disguise unpleasant smells

Exercise L

He became aware of a faint bubbling sound and detected the pungent smell of grease and hot soap from the direction of the kitchen. The kitchen itself stank like a Victorian workhouse laundry. A pail of tea cloths was simmering on an old-fashioned gas stove. In the bustle of departure Dot Moxon must have forgotten to turn off the gas. The gray linen was billowing above the dark, evil smelling scum.

Exercise M

mothballs: spherical camphor balls used to repel insects (moths) in stored clothing; incense: aromatic substances burned for their fragrant odors; lavender: dried parts of lavender flowers used to perfume clothing and rooms

Exercise N (suggestions)

mouth-watering, tasty, delicious, spicy, peppery, scrumptious

18 USING ALL THE SENSES—WHAT DO YOU TASTE? PAGES 72–76

Exercise A

Joanna didn't feel hungry. She continued to sit at the breakfast table looking at her burned toast spread with butter and sickly, sweet raspberry jam. What would she give for something a little bit savory? Maybe a mouth-watering bite of a spicy hamburger with the tang of Spanish onions? Then maybe a rich, medium-rare steak topped with peppery sauce.

Exercise B

(2) Concrete details and April's reaction give a clearer word picture.

Exercise C (suggestions)

salt, bite, condiment, topping

Exercise D (suggestions)

gulp, chomp, chew, sip, suck, gnaw, gobble, lick

Exercise E (suggestions)

tempting, juicy, delicate, sugarless, revolting, stale, tasteless, fresh, bitter, mouth-watering

Exercise F (suggestions)

delicious prawns; tasteless biscuit; hot

(spicy) chicken; stale cake; minty sauce; sour milk

Exercise G

1. wine; 2. Chinese food

Exercise H (suggestions)

weak juice: watery, tasteless; freshly baked bread: mouth-watering, crusty

Exercise I (suggestions)

bland: tasteless, unexciting; unripe: green, immature; sample: taste, try; tart: bitter, tangy; tasty: appetizing, delectable; luscious: delicious, delectable

Exercise J

aftertaste: a taste that lingers in the mouth; taste buds: (elevated) parts of the tongue where taste sensations are experienced; flat: without effervescence (bubbles); sweet tooth: strong liking for sweet foods; masticate: chew thoroughly

Exercise M

nibbling: mice; tearing: bird of prey (eagle); gnawing: rat; pecking: hen; lapping: dog; cracking: parrot

Exercise O

1. makes one feel sick; 2. delicious taste

Exercise P (suggestions)

1. crusty; 2. cheesey; 3. juicy; 4. bubbly; 5. salty; 6. sweet

19 Selecting Direct or Indirect Speech — Pages 77–80

Exercise A

1. Bob said it was his birthday, and he was thirteen.
2. Jillian stated that her family was going to Las Vegas for a vacation.
3. Bill told us we couldn't bring the animals inside.

Exercise B

4. The policeman gave a detailed description of the robbery.

Exercise C

1. agreed; 2. objected; 3. conceded; 4. took offense; 5. concluded; 6. thanked; 7. dismissed; 8. greeted

Exercise E

1. Tony thanked me as I gave him the bat.
2. The producer ordered Sam off the stage.
3. Della gave instructions for fixing the clock.

Exercise F

confirm: agree to the truth or validity; volunteer: offer services, support without request or obligation; insist: express strongly; recite: repeat from memory; dictate: say, report words for transcription

Exercise G

1. threatened; 2. begged; 3. directed; 4. complained; 5. offered

Exercise H

Passage 2

Exercise J

Although Angus's speech would have been interrupted by his eating, the writer has been able to keep the dialogue flowing.

20 Creating Characters — Pages 81–84

Exercise A (suggestions)

1. quiet, loyal, honest, clever
2. cheeky, lively, daring

Exercise C (suggestions)

1. hobble: old man; strut: proud, confident person; dawdle: tired student; prowl: thief; stumble: tired runner; tip-toe: mother at night; 2. questioned: police officer; pleaded: injured person; murmured: person reading; claimed: prisoner; whined: spoiled child; requested: lawyer; 3. peruse: student; glare: annoyed motorist; gape: very frightened person; squint: sentry; investigate: inspector; glance: teacher

Exercise D

Individual responses, for example:

Checklist points	Male character	Female character
Physical appearance	lanky	tall
Movements	slovenly	determined
Behavior to others	rude	respectful
Dialogue	indistinct	snappy
Physical environment	mining town	beach suburb
Character's past	skipped class	sport success
Name	Dan	Cassandra

Exercise E

Oliver Twist: Mrs. Bumble, Artful Dodger; *David Copperfield*: Mr. Peggotty, Mrs. Micawber; *A Christmas Carol*: Scrooge, Tiny Tim

Exercise F

(individual responses, for example) Man–Name: Wilson Jones; Likes: classical guitar, jazz concerts, surfing; Dislikes: magazines, football crowds; Occupation: computer programmer. Woman–Name: Jasmine Rhodes; Likes: Italian food, reading, old movies; Dislikes: sitcoms, cooking, taxi drivers; Occupation: doctor

Exercise G

introvert: private, quiet person; extrovert: outgoing, social person

21 Giving Characters Names Pages 85–88

Exercise A (suggestions)

Ronald, Beryl, Wilma, Ralph, Dorothy, Roger, Doreen

Exercise B (suggestions)

Shorty, Bing, Whacka, Bugsy

Exercise D

Rob, Bob, Bobby, Robbie, Bert

Exercise E (suggestions)

1. Wilfred, Henry, Mervyn; 2. Edith, Gertrude, Sheila; 3. Tracy-Anne, Holly, Meg; 4. Sean, Craig, Andy; 5. Dennis, Matilda, Lorenzo; 6. Lofty, Elfin, Xavier

Exercise G (suggestions)

1. Peter Streeter, Jane Lane, Fay May, Hugh Blue, Ian Green; 2. Bronwyn Brown, Wendy Wilson, Robin Rose; 3. Reed Comic

Exercise H (suggestions)

1. Holly, Jasmine, Lily, Rose; 2. Ginger, Gray, Olive, Violet; 3. Dale, Brook, Cliff, Dell; 4. Mason, Priest, Shepherd, Knight

22 Giving Characters Real Character Pages 89–92

Exercise B (suggestions)

bold: speaks loudly; lazy: leaves clothes on the floor; thoughtless: has to be asked to help with chores; ungrateful: never uses "please"; cheeky: calls people names; disorganized: forgets where he or she left things; selfish: takes the largest piece of pizza; calm: speaks softly, without rushing

Exercise C

1. considerate, anxious, tense;
2. suspicious, upset, agitated, annoyed

Exercise D

(1) *Said* gives little insight into how Margie feels.

Exercise E

1. groaned, chuckled, blurted, snapped;
2. inquired the schoolteacher, giggled her best friend, beamed my mother as she came into my room, boomed the swimming coach, demanded the policeman; 3. "Did your mommy carry your bag?" sneered the bully. "I have an apple for you," beamed the teacher's pet. "Who's next?" called the coach.

Exercise F

the teacher

Exercise G

1. in short sentences, gasps, humming;
2. limp, with a spring, furtively, slyly

Exercise H

bumptious: conceited; meticulous: painstaking, precise about detail; insincere: false; staunch: loyal and dependable; demanding: insisting

Who am I?

Bugs Bunny (among others)

23 Showing, not Telling

Pages 93–96

Exercise A

Most people would find Passage 1 a better example of story writing. It lets the reader use his or her imagination and experiences. The reader is not told everything immediately. The reader's interest is aroused and he or she will want to read on.

Exercise B

1. One answer could be that some motorcycles are trying to get the jump at traffic lights. In that case the writer could have written: The motorcycles waited tensely for the green light.
2. tires spinning

Exercise C

1. a potentially dangerous situation is developing; threatened or surprised.
2. feverish/stressed; water; get things into focus
3. he was afraid, unsure

Exercise D (suggestions)

1. He pulled his collar up around his neck.
2. He nodded his head several times.
3. I stopped suddenly and could feel my ears going red.
4. He plonked down on the sofa and sighed loudly.
5. His arms dropped by his side like lengths of used rope.
6. He shook his head and looked glumly at the ground.
7. His mouth went dry, and there was a sudden ache in the pit of his stomach.
8. She laughed silently and turned away, shaking her head.

Exercise E (suggestions)

1. She sighed softly and her shoulders sagged.
2. "Fool, fool, fool," she muttered to herself.
3. Her shoulder bag was being dragged along like a stubborn puppy.
4. Suddenly, she stopped and with the key just inches from the slot, she looked at the lock.
5. She couldn't wait to get her head on the pillow.

Exercise F

1. tired; 2. agitated/tense; 3. suspicious;
4. amusement; 5. shock

Exercise G (suggestions)

1. The fly zoomed around Ms. Green's lunch box. She tried to flick it away several times.
2. While sitting in the waiting room, Pete watched the second hand of the old wall clock.
3. As he walked home, Jason pulled his shirt out of his trousers.
4. Pauline beamed when she saw her name in the list of competition winners.
5. René rubbed her chin as she watched the kitten at the top of the pole.

24 Selecting a Point of View

Pages 97–100

Exercise A

When <u>I</u> see Marnie, <u>I</u> will tell <u>her</u> that <u>you</u> are staying with an auntie of <u>mine</u>.

Research

1. individual responses; 2. Paul Jennings;
3. Alternate chapters are narrated by the two main characters.

Exercise C

1. first person; 2. third person;
3. third person

25 Finding Other Words for "Say" Pages 101–106

Exercise A

1. annoyance; 2. sadness; 3. regret;
4. amusement

Exercise B (suggestions)

1. "Turn that oven off, now!" ordered the chef.
2. "Oh, I hope it's not another storm coming," moaned the upset camper.
3. The children teased, "We've got your bag. We've got your bag."
4. "But this packet has been opened," complained the customer.
5. "Give it to me!" pleaded the goalie. "I'll clear it to left field."

Exercise D

lecture: lengthy, severe scolding, or informative talk/discourse based on a subject; harangue: loud, forceful, angry speech; blurt: speak/utter suddenly; rave: talk loudly in a wild manner; coax: persuade by flattery/tenderness; interrogate: question closely and insistently

Exercise E

concur: agree, approve; repeat: echo, restate; notify: advise, announce; whoop: cheer, hoot; divulge: betray, disclose

Exercise F (suggestions)

"What have you found?" <u>queried</u> David as Leo stood up.

Leo held a small object up to the light and <u>replied</u>, "It looks like a small gold nugget."

"Can't be," <u>protested</u> David. "This is limestone country."

"Someone might have dropped it," <u>suggested</u> Leo, looking directly at David.

"Yeah, your bank manager!" <u>sniggered</u> David with a smirk.

Leo <u>quipped</u>, "Don't try to be smart. It doesn't suit you."

Exercise G (suggestion)

snarled/demanded

Exercise I

"Let's buy a Harry Potter book for Robert's birthday," suggested Toni.

"I don't think that's a good idea," declared Jenny.

"Why?" asked Toni.

"Because everyone has read all the Harry Potter books," argued Jenny.

Toni shook her head. "The latest Harry Potter book has just been released. It's only been in the stores for two days," she explained.

26 Finding Other Words for "Look" Pages 107–111

Exercise A (suggestions)

2. wistful; 3. curious; 4. furious;
5. concerned; 6. hopeful

Exercise C (suggestions)

1. gazed; 2. inspected; 3. peered at;
4. peek at; 5. studied

Exercise D

browse: look through a book in a casual manner; skim: read in a superficial manner; scowl: have a gloomy or threatening expression; gape: stare in wonder (with mouth open); grimace: have an ugly expression of disgust; gloat: dwell on with evil smugness; behold: look at with regard/wonder

Exercise E

(1), (2)

Exercise F (suggestions)

gaped at, blinked at, stared at, squinted at, watched

Exercise G

frown: glare, glower; review: reassess, examine; investigate: examine, inspect; look up: research, hunt; glimpse: glance, peek

Exercise H

looking daggers: a warning glance; eyeball to eyeball: close confrontation; look-see: check; bird's eye view: view from above

Exercise J

1. She is being secretive/suspicious. 2. He's in love (infatuated) with her.

27 Finding Other Words for "Go" Pages 112–116

Exercise A

2. tired, old; 3. assured; 4. bored; 5. exhausted; 6. laboring; 7. excited, thrilled; (2) is oldest

Exercise C (suggestions)

1. paraded; 2. waded; 3. zoomed; 4. rowed; 5. crawled

Exercise D

promenade: leisurely public walk; twirl: move around repeatedly in a circle, twist, wind; traipse: walk heavily or tiredly, trudge; thread: make one's way through or over something; frolic: dance about light-heartedly; trundle: move heavily; romp: play happily

Exercise E

(3), (4), (1)

Exercise F (suggestions)

bounded, limped, slunk, strutted, swaggered

Exercise G (suggestions)

1. swooped; 2. shadowed; 3. pirouetted; 4. slithered; 5. glided

Exercise H

totter: reel, stagger; trek: hike, tramp; range: roam, wander; lurch: stumble, stagger; escort: accompany, lead

Exercise I

1. walk; 2. drifter/wanderer; 3. travel across the world's oceans

Exercise K

1. She is full of energy and enthusiasm.
2. cautious, timid

28 Structuring a Story 1 Pages 117–121

Exercise A (*The Three Little Pigs*)

Beginning: Three pigs decide to build themselves separate homes. Problem: Wolf likes to eat pigs. Complications: Wolf blows down first and second pigs' homes. They escape to third pig's home. Wolf tries to blow down brick house and fails. Climax: Wolf enters house through chimney. Resolution: Pigs light fire and boil water in huge tub. Wolf dies.

Exercise B (*The Lion and the Mouse*)

Lion catches a mouse and is about to eat it. Mouse pleads for its life and lion relents. Mouse offers to repay lion. Lion laughs. Lion gets trapped in a net and mouse frees lion by gnawing through ropes.

Exercise C

The Ugly Ducking; *The Fox and the Grapes*

29 Structuring a Story 2 Pages 122–129

Exercise A

1. Title: Harley; 2a. Setting (place): family home; 2b. Setting (time): end of summer holidays; 3. Problem: first day at school; 4. Complications: Harley is "accident prone"; 5. Climax: waiting for class dismissal; 6. Coda: Harley ruffles Podgy's ears.

Exercise B

to entertain

Exercise C

long/hot summer; dying grass; brick wall; secret smile; soft/clean sand; new class; big problem; sliding position; surprised yelp

Exercise D

playing dreamily; jumped excitedly; bounced unexpectedly; tricked unfairly; pressed firmly; waited anxiously

Exercise E

Harley; Podgy; Ms. Lambert

Exercise F

1. He was good with animals; 2. tense/grim/ anxious; 3. Harley feeding the goldfish

Exercise G

1. despondent; 2. concerned; 3. liable to become involved in accidents; 4. start of the summer vacation; 5. Where was Harley?; 6. Too late!; 7. self-confident

Exercise H

1. Harley gets a slippery-dip to play on.
2. Harley is given a new bike.
3. Harley overfeeds the goldfish.
4. Harley plays ball with Podgy.
5. Harley's first day at school.

Exercise I

experiences: personal events; U-turn: change direction by 180° or go in the opposite direction; cradled: held tenderly; looming: overshadowing; yanked: sharply pulled

Exercise J

1. surprise; 2. unsure; 3. (over)confident; 4. affection; 5. anguish

Exercise K

yelled, begged, whispered

Exercise L

1. events; 2. He became more assured; 3. He ruffles Podgy's ears; 4. They are more relaxed; 5. individual responses

30 USING METAPHORS, SIMILES, AND CLICHÉS PAGES 130–133

Exercise A

Although the blossoms were as red as blood now, by nightfall they would be like used bandages. Craig wondered if he should have bought plastic flowers. At least they didn't curl up and wilt like cotton candy in the hot sun. Trouble was they looked as phoney as the set of a school play.

Exercise B

Joan's bedroom was a pigsty. In a far corner was a pile of dirty clothes waiting to do battle with any individual who might even consider removing them to the laundry. The hastily discarded school exercise books made a variety of badly built pyramids on her desk. The lonely ceiling light watched with disinterest.

Exercise C

1. Good exam results are a door to future success.
2. The cruel years of toil made the farmer look and feel old.
3. One of the workers was a bull and the other was a lamb.

Exercise D (suggestions)

The beaten dog navigated its way through the crowd to the scrub. The new seedlings wilted sadly in the dry sunshine.

Exercise E

She entered the cabin that was as clean as a beach on a desert island.

Exercise F (suggestions)

as if it were a time bomb; as if it were a delicate piece of china; as if it were stolen treasure

Exercise G

The parade was about to start.

Ken stood as still as a toy soldier (statue). His arms were as stiff as steel rods (power poles) and his head was held high like a guard on duty (proud parent), but his heart sounded like waves on rocks after a storm (a rock band's drummer's solo).

Exercise H

1. railway carriages; 2. train's whistle; 3. individual responses

Exercise I

1. close friends/associates; 2. very upset; 3. living/behaving dangerously; 4. soon going to die; 5. working late

31 Adding Impact with Personification and Hyperbole Pages 134–137

Exercise A

1. The angry sea raged against stubborn rocks. 2. Vines grabbed at Yuri's legs as he stumbled down the hillside.

Exercise B

1. The chili sauce was so hot it left a cinder trail down his throat. 2. Men of iron withstood a never-ending attack of enemy troops.

Exercise C

1. Passage 2; 2. individual responses

Exercise D

1. h; 2. h; 3. p; 4. p; 5. h; 6. p

Exercise E

fairly swarming with goblins, ogres, zombies, and things; gas heater wheezes warnings of doom

Exercise I

My dad is the biggest liar in the whole world. When I was at the bottom of the class in math, he told his friends that I was very close to the top. He can't live with the notion that his only child cannot do a single math question. It makes him madder than an angry bull-ant. All the bull-ants I have come across know more math than I do!

My dad's the local garbage truck driver–and that's the problem. He wants me to have a good education so that I can earn a million dollars before I'm twenty-five. No chance. Even if I did, he'd want me to spend half of it on his sorry old truck. Half the time it's so sick it cannot get up enough enthusiasm to carry an idea half way down our street.

32 Using Different Text Types Pages 138–140

Exercise A

owner has university training, a small business, gives personal attention to customers, has knowledge of older computers

Exercise C

1. young people; 2. It looks like fun; there are lots of things to do; it might be cheap; some of the sideshows might be fake; 3. trying to convince readers that it's full of attractions

Exercise D

historical recount

Exercise E

1. witch/wizard card; 2. school posters

33 Developing a "What if?" Element Pages 141–143

Exercise A

1. The Lion and the Mouse; 2. house/town; 3. lion; 4. in a net

Exercise B (suggestions)

1. What if the tar baby was bubble gum?
2. What if the story was set in the present time?
3. What if Robinson Crusoe was set on an alien planet?
4. What if the mice were pets?
5. What if the island was a uranium deposit?
6. What if the animals were people?
7. What if the Little Red Engine was faint-hearted?
8. What if Robin Hood took place in a modern city?

34 Creating Atmosphere — Pages 144–147

Exercise A

Example 1

Exercise B (suggestions)

Two men in protective clothes stood watching the vulnerable crowd. Two men in circus clothes stood watching the eager crowd.

Exercise C (suggestions)

2. Anders tip-touched the wall. It was as hot as a heat shield.
3. His cape flew out behind him like the wings of a giant bat.
4. A bough fell from an old tree making a crack like a mast collapsing in a strong wind.
5. Alan jumped into the air as if he were in the Olympic Games.
6. The men sat huddled under the umbrella like gnomes under a toadstool.
7. The hare saw the hunter sneaking through the forest like a fox on the prowl.

Exercise D

Many years ago a cunning fox tried to outsmart a wise old owl: fable. The tomb-like room was full of shadows swirling like grey mist: horror. The kitchen stool was harder than any saddle and just about as high: western. The fairy landed on Dana's outstretched arm with a soft flutter: fantasy.

Exercise E

1. isolation
2. the supernatural/fear
3. a grotesque stone face projecting from a roof or gutter

Exercise G

No dim lights from the other cabins punctuated the night. The white man who owned the vast endless fields had scattered cabins of his sharecroppers far apart like flyspecks on a whitewashed ceiling. Sometimes on Sundays the boys walked with their parents to set awhile at one of the distant cabins. Sometimes they went to the meetin' house. And there was school too. But it was far away at the edge of town. Its term began after harvest and ended before planting time. Two successive Octobers the boys had started walking the eight miles mornings and evenings.

36 Looking at the Features of a Story — Pages 149–151

1. a dog that'll be a friend
2. newspaper heading, window sign
3. dogs barking
4. fluffy kittens that Penny stroked
5. like a pom-pom, like a big rat
6. makes the reader wonder what type of friend
7. last line reflects the problem stated early in the story
8. smiled, warned, suggested, explained, asked, declared
9. thoughtful, considerate
10. Slowly selecting his words her father suggested, "There is one place we could try."
11. quiet, calm, thoughtful, determined
12. did not let failure put her off
13. (individual responses)
14. pink blob of curly hair, balloons and streamers covered the window
15. Dogs that could walk on big balls.
16. Arriving at the park they saw lots of dogs with their proud owners.
17. Slowly selecting his words her father suggested, "There is one place we could try."
18. getting a friend/pet dog for Penny
19. looking in the pet store without success
20. Penny becomes more and more disappointed.